Photography
for your family

Better Homes and Gardens

Photography
for your family

MEREDITH PRESS

DES MOINES   NEW YORK

Introduction

Modern cameras are so easy to use that children can take perfect pictures with them. Some cameras feature automatic film transport, instant loading, range finders, and view finders that assure perfect focus and framing, and built-in exposure meters that not only measure the light but also adjust the lenses and shutters for perfect exposures.

What this all means to the amateur photographer is that he can place the emphasis where it belongs. And that is on the picture he is taking rather than on the camera he is using.

Joseph C. Keeley, the author of *Photography for your family* and an amateur photographer for many years, emphasizes pictures and not photographic technicalities. He discusses films and cameras only to the extent necessary to help amateurs get good pictures as well as enjoyment from their cameras, whether new or old. Most of the pictures were taken by amateurs, but some photographs by professionals are used to illustrate picture-taking advice and to show the many different ways to get good pictures from the same situation.

The author recognizes, also, that today's amateur photography (and an amateur is one who takes pictures for the fun of it) is largely color photography, with the shift from black and white accelerated by the breath-taking realism we can now get in color slides and prints. You will find this reflected in pictures that will be as helpful as they are colorful.

Contents

Chapter 1

Little folks

A good photograph of a small child is so prized that more film is used for pictures of babies and children than for any other purpose. The casual photographer, as well as the professional, knows that such pictures are worth shooting for. The rewards certainly are great in the "ohs" and the "ahs" that greet a truly fine picture of this sort.

Today, good pictures of babies and children are much easier to get than they used to be, because of improved cameras, film and lighting equipment. The main reason why parents do not get more outstanding pictures of their children is simply that they don't use their cameras often enough in order to improve their skill.

When to take pictures

There is an almost unlimited range of picture-taking ideas that parents can use in keeping a pictorial record of their children growing up. One idea is to adapt the method horticulturists use to make a photographic record of a growing plant.

Time lapse photography. Setting up a camera (a movie camera is usually used), horticulturists focus on a spot where a seed has been planted, and then secure their camera so there is no chance of movement. Then as hours, days and weeks go by they take pictures at predetermined intervals, a single frame of film at a time. Subsequently, this method gives a film which shows a blade coming through the ground, gradually developing into a plant with stems and leaves, and finally blossoming to full flower.

This is called "time lapse" photography. Parents using the same general idea to depict the growth of their children achieve striking results. One such series has become quite famous, having been used as an advertisement by a major photographic company. The amateur photographer, in this case, took the first picture of his daughter as a baby just starting to walk. Year after year he photographed her in the same spot. The picture story of her life as she grew and developed from a little girl to become a lovely young woman, then a bride and a mother made a fascinating study. Every family photographer could duplicate a series of pictures of this kind. It is quite simple; and actually all you have to do is make certain that you remember to take a picture once a year.

Patience, probably more than technical skill, is needed to get keepsake pictures of children and their pets

Photographing near the water, and in brilliant sunshine, is tricky. Watch exposures so that sun's reflection won't spoil an otherwise perfect picture of a child's romp at the beach.

Special occasions. Each year there are many logical picture-taking days when children play a feature role—Christmas, Thanksgiving, New Year's Day, Halloween, Fourth of July, birthdays and other festive occasions. Birthdays are perfect occasions for the time-lapse series of pictures. The candles on succeeding birthday cakes can provide a visual record of the child's advancing years. There are other big days, also, in the life of a child that should be recorded on film. Don't overlook such religious occasions as christenings and confirmations. Have your camera ready to use when your child starts to walk, when he gets his first haircut or goes off to school for the first time, when special people come to call or when you visit them, or when you have a picnic or go on a trip.

Everyday events. The "little days" in a child's life can provide equally interesting picture possibilities. Consider making a set of pictures that would show a complete day in the life of your child. This series will be interesting at the time it is taken but will become priceless in the years to come. It would portray not just the child as he was, but also his world as it used to be. To make such a record, spend one day with the child, from early morning until bedtime. Record everything that happens. This does not call for a script. Indeed, you should avoid any contrived plot. Show the child asleep in the morning, waking up, being bathed, eating, playing with his toys, his pets, and his friends. You could even show him being reprimanded or spanked, if that becomes necessary. In short, don't miss a thing. You will probably be dead tired at the end of this session but you will have accomplished something.

When you take pictures in sequence you are really telling a story and your approach should be somewhat different. If you want to show a child and a puppy in a single picture you could show them with the youngster holding the pup. On the other hand, a sequence might show the following: (1) pup asleep, (2) boy approaches, (3) boy tickles dog's nose, (4) dog awakes and rolls over on his back to play, (5) boy picks up dog, (6) dog licks boy's face.

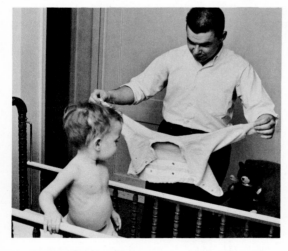

This particular series might never win a prize but it may show how sequence pictures can be more interesting than a single picture. This is particularly true if the pup and the boy are good actors and you are able to capture the young-

Story-telling sequence pictures are highly effective when the star is a child. This off-to-bed series is a good example of the technique and its simplicity. The four pictures—clothes being placed in laundry hamper, hide-and-seek, donning of pajamas, and crib scene—may have little in the way of dramatic plot but they are full of human interest. Such a series of sequence shots, interesting when taken, becomes priceless as time passes.

ster's expressions at precisely the right instant.

The secret of good pictures of children involves more than seeing that your subject is properly lighted and that your camera is sharply in focus. A truly fine picture of a child is one that also captures a cute smile, a look of wide-eyed surprise, a tearful face, a clenched fist, or some other heartwarming manifestation of babyhood. As the baby gets a bit older, your best pictures will be those that relate the child to his new environment— grabbing for a toy, creeping, stuffing food into his mouth, or reaching for his mother.

During these early months, your chances of getting prize pictures will be greatly enhanced if you keep your camera handy, loaded, and ready for use. This does not mean that you must keep it hanging around your neck. Excellent picture possibilities can pass you by, however, if you have to take time out to go upstairs or downstairs to get your camera, only to discover that there's no film in it.

Patience and planning. Before you reach for your camera to take pictures of any small child, even your own, study him for a while. Observe carefully his expressions, his mannerisms, his actions. Some of these will make good pictures, others won't. Decide which you want to try for before you start exposing film, and before you divert him with the sight of the camera.

Sometimes, when you suddenly point a camera at people, big ones as well as little ones, it becomes irresistible. They stare at it, "freeze" and the pictures lose all spontaneity.

There are two ways of dealing with this. Either make the camera as conspicuous as possible, and take (or pretend to take) so many pictures that the subject loses interest in it, or else make it as inconspicuous as you possibly can. In the latter case your aim will be to sneak your pictures without making the camera itself a star attraction.

Professionals do it both ways. Either way they employ a priceless ingredient that the amateur might well consider—patience. Of all the errors that cause poor pictures, many if not most have their roots in impatience. Too many amateur photographers take too many pictures "shooting from the hip." If by chance they have the camera properly set to take the picture, their haphazard shooting is likely to catch the subject in some awkward or inappropriate pose. Take the time to take all of your pictures right.

Any one of these four photographs is outstanding but together, in sequence, they have tremendous impact. The most remarkable aspect of the series, its spontaneity, resulted from the little girl's fascination with what she was doing. By giving a youngster something to do that is more intriguing than the fact that pictures are being taken, you will get photographs with a quality of naturalness seldom obtainable if you rely on coaching.

Where possible, avoid backgrounds that will distract attention from child subject

Simple backgrounds and foregrounds, here provided by sea and sand, put emphasis on the subject

Just as "the play's the thing," so a baby's expression can make the picture a prizewinner

Watch for situations that tell a story. These two candles on the cake spell out a message about the pretty junior miss

Many things are right about this picture. Notable is the angle from which it was shot. A low angle makes viewer participant and provides plain background

People who have made names for themselves as photographers of children never rush an assignment. First of all they take time to study the job to be done. Before they touch their cameras or bring the child on the scene they give careful attention to the setting in which the pictures will be made. They study the lighting and the background and make whatever adjustments are necessary. Preliminaries take time but if you will invest a few minutes in this way it will pay handsome dividends in better pictures.

Importance of light

The most important thing to think about in taking pictures is light; light makes the picture on the film. Your problem as a photographer is to control the light that goes on the film, just as the artist's problem is to apply pigments to canvas to get the effects he desires.

Natural and artificial light. There are two kinds of light; natural light that comes from the sun and artificial or man-made light. You will doubtless take most of your pictures in natural light, but since babies and small children spend a lot of time indoors you'll have to think in terms of artificial light, too, if you want to do justice to your subjects.

Sun and shade. Outdoor pictures are much easier to take than those taken indoors. There are a few things about sunshine that you should know if you want to use it to best advantage for pictures, particularly pictures of small children.

Avoid taking pictures of children in bright sunshine. The brilliant light will make the child squint and is likely to produce harsh shadows. A hazy day will produce better pictures. If you have to shoot on a bright, sunshiny day, try to take your pictures in a shady spot. A word of warning is in order if you are using color. Be careful of the kind of shade you use. Color pictures taken under or near trees often show a greenish tint due to reflection from the leaves. If you take pictures near the side of a red building, the pictures will have a ruddy cast. Sunlight, too, provides definite tints at different times of day. If you shoot color pictures in the early morning hours your slides or prints will have a bluish cast while those made in late afternoon will be on the reddish side. This can provide pleasant effects for certain kinds of pictures but tints of red or blue seldom enhance the pictures of young children. You'll get better results if you try to take your pictures in the late morning and early afternoon hours.

Flash lighting. Many people think that to get good indoor photographs they have to have a lot of elaborate lights, stands, and reflectors. Such equipment can be a handicap when you are taking pictures of small children, providing a distraction far greater than a camera. With any kind of camera you can get by with two or three photoflood lights or a simple flash gun. If you have a camera with a fast lens you can get pictures in any room that is lighted well enough for a person to read comfortably in it.

Available light. When pictures are made indoors without special lighting they are called available-light photographs. They usually have a pleasing, natural quality that is lacking when bright lights or direct flash are used. If you have never tried this kind of photography, do a little experimenting with it. If at first your pictures are underexposed, try again with brighter lights. If you still get underexposed pictures, place your camera on a tripod and try giving the film a longer exposure, Once you have established the kind and amount of light that are needed you will have a highly practical studio at home for all sorts of pictures— and a place where children are likely to act naturally. Another advantage of having a place where you can take pictures under known conditions is that you are not so likely to run across unexpected problems that can spoil pictures that cannot be duplicated.

A good example of what often ruins precious baby pictures may be seen in the maternity ward of virtually any hospital. Invariably, the babies are behind glass windows and quite often the pictures are made with flash, with the results frequently disappointing. If the flash gun is mounted to the camera and the flash is aimed directly at the glass, the finished picture will almost certainly show a large blob of white instead of a baby because the brilliant flash will have been reflected from the glass into the camera lens.

To avoid this, if your flash gun can be removed from the camera, angle it so that the flash hits the glass obliquely. Play it safe by taking several pictures. Also, be sure to focus your camera carefully. The closer you get to your subject the less leeway you have in this respect. The technical term for it is "less depth of field." All you have to remember is that if the baby is five feet away from you, focus your camera at five feet; not six or seven, if you want good, sharp pictures.

Because of the importance of the occasion, you might use a tripod. With this accessory you won't have to use flash at all, as new babies will usually oblige by lying still long enough for fairly long exposures. Another advantage of the tripod is that you can focus more carefully. The distance from your camera to the bassinet will remain constant, letting you get better pictures.

Since it is urgent that you get a picture of Baby at this point, don't stop trying when you've taken some pictures of him in the observation gallery. Most hospitals permit the baby to be photographed in the room with its mother, and you will certainly want to be sure and get pictures showing the two top stars.

There is no need for elaborate lighting equipment when you want to take pictures of your children in your home. If you believe that the regular room lighting is insufficient, adding inexpensive photofloods will do the job.

A flash gun will stop action, even of an active boy and his dog. Here, the subjects were kept away from wall at rear, picture was taken from above eye level and session was brief.

This is another kind of twosome that can make grist for the photographic mill, but in this case the expression of the boys and the composition of the picture produced results vastly different from the self-conscious photographs that remind one of the old-fashion "watch the birdie" days.

Lighting is important in any kind of portraiture. Made by the light of a window, this picture was much improved with a reflector, used to lighten the left side of the child's face.

Children can provide a wealth of picture possibilities as they discover and adjust to the strange new world about them

Circus days are bound to be festive times for all youngsters. They will give you many opportunities for colorful shots

Simple props in simple settings often help you get outstanding pictures. But keep in mind that your subject is not the prop but the child

*Changing seasons multiply picture
possibilities, and fall with its
bright harvest of colors gives you
a chance for pictures like this*

*Lighting helped make this picture. Note
how sun comes over little girl's
shoulder. Had she faced the sun there
would have been strong shadows*

*Of all the holidays of the year none
approaches Christmas for photos
of children. On that day load up with
film, be ready for anything*

Flash-bulb protection. Be careful if you use flash bulbs. That brief flash of light won't hurt the baby's eyes but occasionally a bulb will shatter. You can prevent the possibility of injury by using a flash guard. Small plastic envelopes like those used in the kitchen will serve very well to guard the bulb or the reflector. A handkerchief will also work and it will diffuse the light.

Using a handkerchief draped over a reflector is recommended for pictures of anyone, not just babies. Even the tiniest flash bulbs pack a lot of concentrated light and unless they are used with discretion the pictures can be too contrasty and disappointing because of their chalk-and-charcoal effect. Flash can also cause unsightly shadows when the subject is close to a wall. To prevent those hobgoblin background effects there's a simple remedy—move the subject a few feet away from the wall. The change in angle may make the shadow disappear completely. If it should still show up it won't be so prominent.

Wherever possible avoid shooting down when you are taking photographs of children. Results will be far more natural if you can snap the pictures at their level.

This is especially important as children grow and are able to be on their own. Then, they make possible the best pictures of all as they "work" at being kids. That is when you can catch them playing and squabbling together, discovering such wonders as birds and bugs, and otherwise enjoying and adjusting to the strange world about them. As you watch them from the side lines, be prepared for anything that may happen but keep in mind that it is likely to happen fast. Photo-graphically speaking, that is going to call for shutter speeds of 1/100th of a second or faster and quick reflexes on your part.

It is assumed that you know enough about your camera so that you understand how to use it and don't attempt any pictures that are beyond its limitations. If you have a box camera, or some other type with a slow lens, don't try to take indoor pictures without flash or ample floodlighting. Also, it probably won't permit you to get very close to the subject without a close-up lens attachment; so don't try. A handy accessory for such a camera is a simple tape measure. If the instructions with the camera say that the minimum working distance is six feet and you want to get as close to the subject as possible, measure six feet. Most people are poor judges of distance so, to be on the safe side, don't guess.

Bracketing. A good understanding of the properties of film and how to use it is excellent insurance against poor pictures.

Helpful, also, in assuring that you get the pictures you want is a technique used by professionals called bracketing exposures. When a professional wants to make sure of getting a perfectly exposed shot, he first takes a reading of the light level with an exposure meter. But he doesn't take just one picture based on the exposure recommended by the meter. He takes some extra pictures, varying the exposures to give a little more and a little less exposure to the film. He does this to make absolutely sure of getting the finest possible picture. There is no need for the amateur to do this every time he takes pictures, but for the

You'll need a camera with a fast shutter speed, good vantage point and fast reflexes if you want to make sure that you stop the action, catch story-telling grimaces of the young athletes in your neighborhood.

Some of the finest pictures of children are those that show them as they fit themselves to their environment. Be prepared for anything as you watch from sidelines but keep in mind that it is likely to happen rapidly.

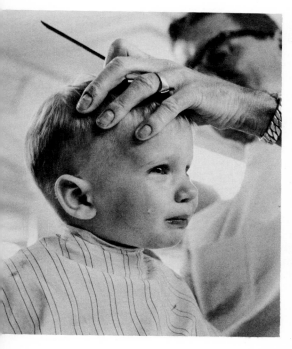

It may not be a holiday, officially, but a very important event in the life of a very young man is when he gets his first haircut. This event is another occasion well worth filming.

Keeping an active youngster in one place is always a problem for a photographer. A highchair is helpful in such cases but sometimes, as here, the background is "too busy," detracts from good picture.

As children grow older, getting pictures of them can become more strenuous. However, the results you get can justify the effort, especially if you are able to snap such candid action shots as this one.

truly important pictures bracketing can be good insurance for getting satisfactory pictures.

Inevitably when discussing photography it becomes necessary to pay some attention to the mechanics of a camera, but all too often such discussions become overly technical for the average person. Actually there is little need for technical talk. The important thing is to know what your camera will do and what it won't do. You can get a good idea of its capabilities and limitations if you study your camera and the instruction book that came with it. You can put this information to practical use by taking, with care, as many pictures as possible.

There is an important follow-through necessary in photography just as there is in golf or trapshooting. After you have taken pictures of your new baby, which turn out well because you were careful to take them properly, don't stop at this point. Follow through with identifying each slide or print fully. Record the date it was taken, where it was taken, and the names of those who appear in it. You may think this is superfluous, since surely you will remember such things as these. But a few years hence questions are bound to come up. Was this Jean or was it Peggy? Was Bobby six years old when this was taken? Who was that girl holding Jimmy? Was this taken at Thanksgiving or was it Christmas? Play safe and get the information down as soon as you get the slides or prints back from the processor. Some day you'll be glad you did.

When taking a snow scene such as this, be careful of exposure. Bright sunlight reflected from snow can result in overexposed pictures. Use a light meter but take the reading from faces, not snow.

The child's exploring finger, as he gets his first lesson about fish, makes this picture. Such gestures happen quickly so be ready for them

Chapter 2

Big people

In the early days of photography, it was an easy matter to get a picture of your family or a group of friends. All you had to do, if the sun was shining brightly, was to line them up, facing the sun, with the tall ones in the rear and the shorties up front. Then, with a reminder not to squint or laugh, you gave them time to fix their faces in the proper expression. After peering into the finder, if they all were present, you pushed the button.

The resulting picture may have lacked spontaneity but it showed Uncle Will, Aunt Sarah, and assorted cousins so that they were recognizable. Subsequently, it was pasted down as a minor masterpiece in the family album.

You can still take pictures like that; many people do. With pioneer photographic equipment, you almost had to take static snapshots. This was true if it was necessary to show a number of subjects in a single picture. The film that was available then was not very sensitive and bright sunlight was necessary, particularly when box cameras and folding cameras with inferior lenses were used. Another limiting factor was the slow shutter speeds of most early cameras. If your subjects showed much animation, your picture would have been marred by blurs. Little wonder that the key phrase was, "hold it!"

Today, most of the tens of millions of cameras in use have no such limitations. There is no longer any reason for lining your subjects up as though they were facing a firing squad. Get people to act at ease. You'll get more pictures you like if people act natural. Let them sit around a table, or at a fireplace, and relax. Give them something to eat or drink; anything to free them of the notion that they are supposed to watch the birdie. Your pictures will be far better than the gay nineties group pictures and you will get more satisfaction out of taking and showing them.

When taking photographs of individuals, you can help make them act more natural and spontaneous by the use of appropriate props. Suppose you want to get a picture of your friend, Jim, who lives down the street. Jim is a rugged outdoor type who loves to hunt and fish. You could take Jim's picture in a business suit or even in a dinner jacket but this would be out of character since it wouldn't show the Jim that everybody knows. To get *that* Jim, have him dress informally and be cleaning his shotgun or working on his fishing tackle. Or get him outdoors with game he has just bagged or a fish he has caught.

Likewise, a picture of Sam Smith, the neighborhood druggist, can be made more meaningful if

Years ago, when a family was photographed it was a serious occasion and the subjects showed it

Nowadays, the aim of a family photo is to show members as they really are, natural and unposed. In such pictures the camera is ignored as the subjects relax and attempt to be themselves.

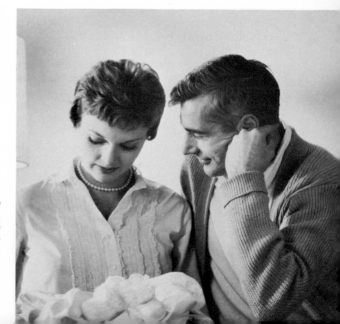

you snap him behind his prescription counter pouring medicine from a graduate into a bottle, or weighing some powder on his scales. You could take Mother's picture showing her at ease in a rocking chair, in the pose made famous by Mrs. Whistler. It might be however, that Mother is an excellent golfer; in which case a far more natural picture would show her hitting a long drive down the fairway or sinking a putt.

Not only do such touches give an additional dimension to your pictures, they are likely to put the subject at ease so that your pictures look more natural. In familiar surroundings, doing the things they like to do, people are more spontaneous in their actions. It helps, too, if you can get them to talk about their interests, or demonstrate them. If you are taking pictures of Jim the outdoorsman while he is cleaning his gun and ask him something about the accuracy of his firearm or how it works; he'll probably forget all about the camera while he answers your question. And that is your chance to catch the real Jim. This is simply applied psychology, as practiced by top-ranking photographers who specialize in taking pictures of people.

One word of caution. Keep in mind that you are taking a picture of Jim, not his beloved fishing tackle or his trusty firearm. Never subordinate the subject to the prop.

Big people as well as little folks enjoy holidays and other days when something special is going on; such as a wedding, an anniversary, a family reunion, a graduation. These occasions provide excellent picture possibilities. When you are taking pictures at such affairs don't separate the people from the proceedings. At a graduation, the star of the show could be photographed receiving his diploma, or talking to his teachers, or showing his parents around the school. At a family reunion, photograph the people reminiscing together at the dinner table, or playing games, or dancing. Wait to snap your pictures until everyone is relaxed and doing something that will add more meaning to the picture.

Admittedly, this is extra work. You'll have to sacrifice some of your time, and some of the fun, to take pictures. But the result will be worth the extra effort; particularly when you get around to re-enacting the event with a showing of interesting slides or outstanding prints. On that occasion, the spotlight will definitely be on you.

Plan ahead before you shoot

There are several things to remember whether you are taking pictures of one person or many. Think in terms of the finished picture and how it will look. There is the simple matter of whether you should take your picture as a horizontal or a vertical. Unless you are using a camera such as a twin-lens reflex that gives you a square format, this can be most important. A head shot of a person obviously calls for a vertical format; unless you are purposely striving for some unusual effect. A horizontal picture is indicated if you are taking a picture of a person lying on a diving board or in a hammock. Yet some people never give this aspect a second thought and they take all of their pictures either one way or the other.

Dress for the occasion. Another oversight, and one that causes many pictures to be discarded, is so elementary that many camera-users never think of it until it is too late. That is, when you are taking pictures of people, allow them to make themselves presentable. Women don't appreciate a picture showing their hair in curlers or without any make-up whatsoever. Few men are likely to care much for a picture that emphasizes their bald spots or their midriff bulges.

Again, unless you are striving for a special effect, hair should be combed and brushed, ties straightened, faces washed, unsightly bulges and wrinkles in clothing smoothed, and women should apply necessary make-up. Don't overdo it, however. You want pictures of your friends as they are, looking neither sloppy nor overly prettified, and dressed properly for the occasion, and for the setting in which they happen to be. If they are bowling, it would be out of place to present them as though they were attending the country club's annual cotillion.

Thought should also be given as to where you as the photographer should stand in relation to your subject; whether you should be close up or at some distance away. Here, too, it is most important to think in terms of the finished picture. If you want to fill the frame of your pictures with a person's head or his head and shoulders, without including a lot of extraneous material, you will have to get close when using a normal lens. However, if that extraneous matter is important to the picture, move back far enough to include it. This may seem elementary but many amateurs persist in shooting most of their pictures from a distance that is usually too far away to give correct emphasis to the center of attraction.

You can improve your chances of getting good pictures of people if you learn to use your camera's view finder properly; whether it is a simple peephole or the most advanced reflex type.

Another important thing to consider, once you have the subject properly centered in the finder and the camera is not tilted, is the background. Is that tree in the landscape situated so that its branches are going to jut out of your subject's ears in the finished slide or print? Is that neon sign going to spell out its message right over his head? Also, what about the person's appearance? Will his necktie be askew? Will his face show a five o'clock shadow? Too often, these questions are answered only in the finished pictures. You can get the answers beforehand if you use your camera's view finder properly. It may take as

Two or more photoflood lights with built-in reflectors permit you to try your hand at portraits, studio style. Use a plain background. This effect is what you get with just one light, directed head-on at the model. Results are like those obtained with a camera-mounted flash.

By the use of two lights, as was done here, the shadows that marred the portrait at the left were lightened considerably. To get this picture, one light was placed above and to the left of the subject and then the second light added was placed at the right, and at eye level.

With the use of a third light you can add interesting touches. The above picture used the basic lighting of the picture at upper right while the third light was aimed at the subject's hair from above. Halo effect enhances picture, gives more separation from background.

To achieve an added professional effect you may want to add a fourth reflector spot to the three-light setup used in the picture at the left. The fourth light was placed above the model's head and behind her and the light directed on background for still more separation.

Master using camera view finder and you'll improve chances of getting good pictures of people

Today's color film accurately reproduces the beauty of outdoor scenes

Take your time composing pictures. Decide how much you want to include. Study light, shadow

*This picture of a happy angler
has extra meaning because
it shows all pertinent details*

*Settings that relate to picture
subject can add meaning.
Don't let setting dominate shot*

*Should picture be horizontal
or vertical? Upright figure
and poles provide the answer here*

much time as the old-time photographer used to take studying the ground glass of his view camera under a canopy of heavy black cloth, but it will be time well spent.

If you really study the view finder you'll find that you can also learn a great deal about light, which is the basis of all photography. You'll be able to see how brilliant sunlight can give sparkling pictures, but at the same time mar them with deep shadows. You can see how the light of an overcast day can give more attractive flesh tones, without the bright patches and dark shadows that come from brilliant sunlight. A simple demonstration such as this is important for anyone who wants to get good pictures of people.

Experiment with light sources

If light is improperly utilized, whether its source is from the sun, floodlights, flash bulbs or electronic flash, the picture results will be disappointing. As an experiment with indoor lighting, take one picture with the flash gun attached to the camera. You will get a brilliantly lighted picture. However, it is likely to be so uniformly bright that the subject's face will be washed out and flat. If you remove the flash from the camera and hold it above and to one side of the camera you will get a better picture. It won't be so flatly lighted but shadows will become apparent, sometimes to the detriment of the picture subject. However, if you aim your flash at a near-by ceiling or wall in order to get a reflected light, that is referred to as bounce light, you will be getting an effect similar to the lighting you get outdoors on a hazy day—and a better picture is likely to result.

Lighting is fundamental in all photography and is particularly so in portraiture—whether candid or formal. Whenever light comes from a single source, natural or artificial, you may get too much light in one area and too little in another. So you need to learn how to balance it. Using flash or strobe you can do this by means of reflected or bounce light, which spreads the light more evenly. However, it is not always possible to use this method.

One of the oldest and most effective methods to spread light is to use reflectors. Professionals use elaborate frames covered with reflecting material, but for the amateur a sheet of white cardboard will serve. Place the cardboard so that some of the bright light falling on and near the subject is reflected to brighten up the shadowy spots. This is a good way to make the light level fairly uniform and provide some shadow, but not enough to be objectionable.

Key lights and fill lights. Another means of achieving balance when using artificial light, is to use more than one light source. Portrait photographers rarely use a single light, and do so only when they want a special effect. In order to make a subject as attractive as possible, they use two, three, or more lights.

Certain basic patterns are followed for portrait lighting. If you like to experiment, the field is wide open. The main light source is called the key light and other lights modify it. The key light may be used to provide flat lighting from the front, close to the camera, or it may be used from a height or from the side or even from the rear of the subject. The secondary light, called a fill light, is not so bright and is usually placed at a greater distance from the subject. It lightens the shadows produced by the key light. By shifting the lights around you can get all sorts of effects.

You need not stop with just two lights. You can add as many as you wish. If you go beyond three or four you are likely to complicate matters needlessly. These additional lights, though, can produce interesting touches. Some photographers use these supplementary lights to brighten the background or they shine them on the subject's hair or they may be used to accent the hands or lighten some shadow areas.

This sort of portraiture photography does not call for the expensive lighting equipment found in commercial studios. You can get by without reflectors or light stands, as often two, three, or four photoflood bulbs with built-in reflectors will do the job. Used in fixtures which have movable sockets or a flexible column, these lamps permit you to turn any room into a portrait studio. For much of your work, you can probably get ample light from two or three 100- or 150-watt bulbs. These conventional bulbs, however, do not have the reflector feature and you cannot concentrate the light exactly where you want it.

Still another kind of light that can give you excellent portraits is flash, either the conventional type or electronic. For best results, two or three flash units are necessary. They need to be wired so that they will go off simultaneously. This kind of setup has the advantage of permitting you to stop action, no matter how fast, or to catch a fleeting expression. It is harder to control than photoflood lighting. You cannot be completely sure of how the light will balance or where the shadows are likely to fall, unless you first check out your lighting setup with photofloods. After checking, substitute flash at identical places.

If your camera is the type that lets you see results of picture taking in seconds, you can quickly decide if you need to correct something and then take other shots

28

Chapter 3

Animal kingdom

He who points a camera at his cocker spaniel or Siamese cat, he who takes pictures of animals in the woods or in a zoo, is doing what has come naturally to man for countless centuries. Look for evidence in caves and tombs where ancient man carved or sketched likenesses of the birds and beasts he saw around him, creatures that shared his burdens or threatened his existence.

This consuming interest in animal life is as great today as it was in the distant past, and it's a fact that is well known to practical students of human behavior. Editors are aware that a good picture of a winsome puppy or kitten is an attention-getter that is second only to an illustration of an appealing youngster or a lovely young woman. Advertising men know that a sure-fire way to make certain that people read their message is to embellish it with an eye-catching illustration of an animal.

With reasonable care anyone can take good animal photographs, but it is not enough to get pictures that are good from a technical standpoint only. Your aim should be to show the animal as he is, natural and unposed, with his personality showing. If you own a pet, or if you love animals, it is hardly necessary to point out that animals are highly individualistic, with distinctive personalities that they show in various ways. It's up to you, the photographer, to capture on film the animal's dignity, its clownishness, its ferocity, its gentleness, any of its other characteristics you discover.

Success with household pets. You can help to set the stage to get such pictures if you prepare the animals properly and place them in the proper setting. If you own a fine Persian or Siamese cat, or a show animal, you should have her properly preened for pictures. However, if your cat happens to be a veteran of many alley wars, by all means show him with his battle scars, and try to catch that bellicose glare. If you can coax him to bare his fangs and arch his back, so much the better. You may then find that you have a prize-winning picture.

If you are a dog fancier, the same principle applies. A show dog should be photographed in all his dignity, cleaned, trimmed, and brushed. A field dog appears at his best in his natural element, pointing game or retrieving it. If your dog is clever, show him doing his tricks. If he's a clown, photograph him when he's at his best "hamming it up."

While the emphasis here has been on dogs and cats, don't neglect other pets that you may have or which you can photograph in the homes of friends. Canaries, parrots, and pigeons make good subjects, and parakeets are even better because they are easily trained to perform within camera range outside a cage. The kind of pets fancied by children—guinea pigs, hamsters, white mice, turtles, and snakes—are excellent subjects but for this kind of photography special equipment is necessary since such pictures must be taken at very close range. Your best bet is to use

Pets can be skittish one minute, docile the next. Coax rather than command for best results

You can quite often get close-up shots of wildlife, without a telephoto lens, if you stalk your quarry cautiously.

You may sometimes need an assistant to get the picture you want. Here, the photographer put a basket over the kittens to keep them quiet while he adjusted his camera. As helper lifted basket, picture was snapped.

On most occasions it will be difficult, at best, to get pets to pose at your bidding. Be alert to those off-guard moments that reflect most appealingly a pet's dignity, or his clownishness, or other characteristic.

a camera that, by means of a bellows or extension tube, allows you to work within a few inches, but lacking this you can get a close-up lens which, slipped over your regular lens, permits you to work at close range.

This sort of photography, however, is primarily for the sedentary. If your preferences run to the outdoors you have a veritable Noah's Ark of subjects to choose from. A short drive will probably bring you to a farm where a polite request will usually get you permission to shoot pictures to your heart's content. State and county fairs provide a bonanza of prize livestock of all kinds, and if you are looking for thoroughbred horses you'll find them at shows, at racetracks, riding schools, and dude ranches.

Zoo photography. To photograph wild animals, you can find much to keep you busy at circuses and at roadside animal farms, but your best bet is likely to be a near-by zoo. Nowadays zoo photography is far more interesting than it used to be because modern zoos keep many animals in outdoor surroundings instead of in cages; pictures are therefore more natural looking. Here a few pointers will help you take full advantage of these conditions. You can stroll through the zoo and take snapshots as you go, during brief pauses. However, if you take enough time to work yourself into a choice location and then wait for the animals to do something interesting, the pictures you get will be far better.

If you want to get the best possible pictures, enlist the help of zoo attendants. They can direct you to the spots where the best performers may be found, they can arrange to place you in the most advantageous position, and they may even be able to stimulate some action on the part of the animals. In return you can give them, or the zoo itself, some of the pictures you take; this can pave the way to get other and possibly even better animal pictures.

In any case, when you go to the zoo, find out about the rules and regulations and obey them. In most zoos, photographers are encouraged and are given every opportunity to get good pictures, but this does not give the person with a camera a license to annoy other visitors or the animals with boorish behavior. The person who wants to get good pictures will visit the zoo only on days when visitors are not out in force. On such days, the rules regulating the use of tripods and flash pictures are likely to be least stringent, you will be able to pick the best locations with the least difficulty. The animals can be encouraged more easily to pose for you rather than for a multitude of other photographers.

Even though the trend is to the use of open, moated enclosures or glass-fronted cages, it is necessary on many occasions to cope with the problem of shooting your pictures through steel bars or wire mesh. If you want to have the bars or mesh show in your pictures stand back at least two feet, and there will be no mistaking the fact that you are taking a picture of a caged animal, particularly if you are using a small lens aperture. On the other hand, if you wish to get a good animal picture unadorned by a geometrical pattern in the foreground, place your camera as close to the cage as you can with safety. If you are up against bars, they may be far enough apart so that the lens will be clear of any obstructions, though this is not likely to be the case with wire mesh. Still, it won't matter if you can get your lens within a foot or so of the mesh. Taking your pictures thus, using as wide a lens opening as possible, the wire will not be apparent in the finished picture. But be careful. Don't get yourself in a position where a hairy paw can slash at you or your camera. If you want to play safe, have a talk with one of the keepers before you try for any such pictures. Quite often a keeper will locate a safe spot for you, and then act as guardian while you take your pictures.

Exposure meter helps. One helpful accessory for the person who goes in for zoo photography is an exposure meter. That is because so many different kinds of lighting are encountered. One moment you will find yourself taking pictures of a polar bear in brilliant sunlight, enjoying himself in a pool of water, and the next minute you may be inside trying to get pictures of monkeys in a cage. Your eyes adjust quickly to tremendous variations in light, and few people are able to guess changing light levels with much accuracy. It is noteworthy that seasoned professionals don't try to guess. They make sure by checking the light with an accurate meter. You, too, will find it a good investment, one that pays off in better

pictures and less wasted film.

If you are willing to make the effort, you can find material for excellent animal and bird pictures in your own back yard. Not much effort is required but patience is necessary to get good photographs of the birds, squirrels, chipmunks, rabbits and other wildlife that are found almost everywhere. One means of getting interesting photographs is a feeding station, or several stations. Once the birds and the animals start using them your work is simplified. In time, if you mind your manners, they may accept you as "one of the club," and you can photograph them to your heart's content.

Better animal photography

Photographing timid wild things takes time but two short cuts will help you get the picture you want. One is a camera which has a telephoto lens, which permits you to shoot them from a distance. Lacking that, it is not difficult to rig up devices that permit you to manipulate your camera from a distance. The simplest is a string attached to the release lever of a box camera, or one of the other simple types that permits such usage. For a more advanced camera, a long cable release will permit you to place your camera close to a strategic spot while you keep a respectable distance. Or, if you want something more elaborate, your camera dealer can show you how to get your pictures at a distance using flash. In this case you can either shoot the picture yourself or set up a device that causes the animal to take his own picture by tripping a wire.

If you would prefer to go hunting for pictures instead of venison or goose, your procedure will be rather similar to that of the hunter with a

Miniature pets such as turtles can make interesting picture subjects. However, in order to photograph them successfully you must work at close range. A close up lens permits you to work within a foot or so of the subject. If your camera is a type that will take a bellows or extension tubes, close up work can be very rewarding.

The setting of an outdoor zoo resembles animals' natural habitat. Here, you can get virtually the same pictures you'd get on big game hunting safari

You needn't hurry in taking pictures at a zoo. With captive subject, you can try again for the right shot

A short drive out in the country will probably bring you to a farm where a polite request will get you permission to shoot pictures of your children and farm animals

This picture required more than an hour of patient waiting. Shutter was released at precise moment to catch peak of dog's uncertainty as to his next move

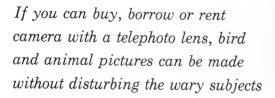

If you can buy, borrow or rent camera with a telephoto lens, bird and animal pictures can be made without disturbing the wary subjects

Ask zoo director to direct you to spot where best performers are to be found. Wait for desired action

firearm. He goes where game is likely to be, he stalks it carefully, and he tries not to make his presence known. Even though he may not be a very good hunter he may come upon a fine buck or a fat pheasant (in season, of course), by sheer luck. And so may you. If you get a break like this, be ready to take advantage of it. Your quarry is not likely to stop and pose for you so be prepared by having your camera properly set and the shutter cocked. It's a good habit to acquire anyway. Some of the finest pictures ever made have been those that were shot on the spur of the moment.

Animal photography poses a few problems that the amateur should recognize, not only to get better pictures of animals but to give him a better understanding of photography generally. A good example of this deals with the manner in which your eye sees things differently from the camera. For one thing, the human eye sees things in three dimensions, whereas the picture you get from your camera appears on a flat surface. However, the big difference lies in the way the eye and the camera see things. You might say that they have a different viewpoint in that the camera sees the world in an *objective* manner and records quite literally the things it sees. By way of contrast the human eye sees things selectively. It takes in everything but the human eye

concentrates on certain objects that are of special interest to the viewer.

What this means when you are taking a picture of an animal can be readily understood. Let's say your dog is romping on the lawn and you decide to film his antics. But when the pictures come back from the processor you are disappointed. The dog is so small that he's lost in a large expanse of lawn. Don't blame the camera; it was your eyes and your brain that tricked you. They were aware of all that grass but they subordinated it to the image of the dog that you wanted to see, so they provided an effect similar to that of a telephoto lens, enlarging the image of the dog in your own mind. The camera, with no special interest in your dog, presented a different version.

What is the solution to this vexing problem? Actually there are three solutions. Professional photographers and advanced amateurs get close-up pictures of animals from a distance by using long-focus or telephoto lenses. Obviously such lenses are essential in photographing wildlife from a distance but they make it easier to get good pictures of pets, too, since dogs and cats become as self-conscious as humans when a camera lens is poked at them.

Since relatively few amateurs own cameras with telephoto lenses, however, they must look for other solutions. The simplest is to get as close

Cropping a picture enables you to make dramatic changes in what might otherwise be an ordinary photograph. You can enlarge certain portions of the negative but retain the original format. You can alter the shape, making it either a horizontal or a vertical. The picture above, taken with a box camera, originally had a square format. Cropping it as a vertical (at right) enlarges the animals somewhat but places more emphasis on the tree. Changing the format to a horizontal (opposite page) puts more emphasis on animals.

to your subject as possible, so he doesn't turn up as a speck in the finished print or transparency. This poses no problem if you are taking pictures of a large animal such as a horse or a cow. In that case the animal's bulk will fill the frame of the picture. But a dog or cat is relatively small so you will have to get pretty close to him. If your camera is like so many, with a minimum range of six feet, you will probably find that this brings the image of your pet to adequate size, and if you want to get more of a close-up picture you can do so by adding an inexpensive supplementary lens, usually referred to as portrait lens.

Cropping. Another way of increasing the size of the subject in a finished picture is one that doesn't occur to most amateurs, though it is a method that professionals use as a matter of course. They seldom use the entire picture they take but crop or delete parts of it, sometimes most of it, to emphasize what they want emphasized. If you take a black and white picture in which your pet is too small it's a simple matter to obtain an enlargement of just the part of the negative in which he appears. Doing so with a color transparency is a bit more complicated but processors will do the job on order.

However, if you use your camera with understanding it won't be necessary to call for special services from your photo-finisher. In the case of animal photography "understanding" means more than a knowledge of the camera itself, its capabilities and its limitations. It also means a certain *rapport* with your subject. This is every bit as important in getting pictures of animals as it is with children, and it calls for at least as much patience. You are not likely to get good, spontaneous photographs of dogs and cats by angry commands or threatening gestures.

The hardest problem facing the photographer is to persuade an animal to pose properly without seeming to pose. Most animals become restive when they are required to stay in one place very long and it doesn't help if you lose patience and try to force him to remain where he is. If your pet shows that he's tired of having his picture taken, give him a recess, play with him, and give him a toy or tidbit to get him back in the mood. If the animal is not yours you will probably have to exercise even greater patience.

In any case, the sessions will have to be short and that means you should be prepared to get your pictures quickly. Decide where you are going to place the animal, making sure that there is no unsightly background, measure the distance carefully, and focus your camera accordingly. Check the light and decide on the exposure you are going to use. Then lead your pet onto the set

and you will be prepared for whatever performance he chooses to give or which you can possibly coax out of him.

This may call for a more methodical approach to picture-taking than you are accustomed to, but there is a special reason for all this care when you are taking close-up pictures of a dog, cat, or other pet. The closer you get to the subject you are photographing the more critical you have to be in focusing. At a distance of 50 feet or 25 feet you have considerable leeway with regard to focus, but as the distance between camera and subject lessens you have to be increasingly careful. Under certain conditions—at extremely close distances of two or three feet when large lens apertures are used—the depth of field, or sharpness range of the picture, may be only a matter of a few inches.

This is important; the hallmark of a fine animal photograph is its sharpness of detail, with hairs and head details showing as crisp and distinct as a fine etching. You may think that results such as these are obtainable only by specialists in animal photography, using the finest equipment, but any camera used with understanding can produce such results. Each year additional proof of this is given in the form of prize-winning pictures made by teen-agers who more often than not use run-of-the-mill cameras.

Distortion. In photographing pets at short range, another basic fact about photography soon becomes apparent. This has to do with distortion. Keep a respectable distance from the person or thing you are photographing, and you will get little or no distortion. In the photographic scheme of things distance lends not enchantment but perspective, so that everything looks natural when you look at the picture you take. But let's say you photograph a friend at a distance of only five feet and he extends a hand toward the camera. That distorted hand will dominate the picture and spoil it for you.

Unless you are careful when you photograph an animal close-up you are likely to get a somewhat similar effect. If you photograph a dog head-on his muzzle will appear large and misshapen, while his eyes and head will recede unnaturally into the background. To avoid this, don't get too close to him, and take your pictures from an angle that will keep the animal's head in the proper perspective. In other words, if you feel you want to get an extreme close-up, make sure that the animal's nose is not pointing directly at the camera, especially if, like a collie or a German shepherd, it has a long nose.

This is a good thing to keep in mind when you are taking pictures of people, too. Extreme close-ups can be effective but if they are not taken with discretion and with some knowledge of this quirk of photography, you can end up with undesirable results.

When an animal is your subject you must be prepared at all times for its sudden movement. Because of this you should use the fastest shutter speed that you can, particularly if you are trying for a picture in which the animal is expected to do something anyway. A cat reaching out for a catnip mouse is likely to do so with a quick jab of its paw rather than a leisurely swing, and a dog usually moves rapidly when a ball or a biscuit is thrown his way. Unless you want to show a blur, fast shutter speeds are essential.

This can present a problem, especially if you are working where the light is poor, but flash offers a practical solution. Indeed it is sometimes a good idea to use flash even when taking pictures of animals in daylight. The reason is that when you take flash pictures close-up you must necessarily use a small lens opening so you don't overexpose. This automatically serves to give you all the depth of field you are likely to need for sharpness, and in addition you can use a fast shutter speed. Whatever kind of light you are using, be sure to provide more of an exposure if the animal has dark fur. A black cocker spaniel, for example, will show up in a picture looking like a silhouette unless you open up the lens enough to register detail.

By using flash when photographing animals close up, in daylight, you get depth of field needed for sharpness.

A fast lens can stop the action
of swiftest animal. Food, as
a bribe, usually brings the most
timid animal in camera range

Chapter 4

Close to home

To most amateur photographers, homes are merely backgrounds for pictures of people and things, and rarely if ever are they starred in their own right. Granted, not everyone's home is as attractive as those that you are likely to find featured in leading national magazines but a pictorial record of your home is important to you for several worth-while reasons.

One reason is a sentimental one. Few people today spend all their lives in one house, and it is good to have sets of photographs showing where you have lived; not just pictures of the houses themselves but also of the communities. Even if you do remain in the same house all your life, pictures of it are important to give you a record of the changes over the years of both your home and the community.

How to photograph your home. An even better reason for taking such pictures, however, is that a project of this sort can be fun if you go about it properly. The proper way is not to walk out to the street, center the house in your viewfinder and then snap the picture. That's the way most people take pictures of their houses and that is why so many such pictures are uninteresting, at best, and why some are so badly distorted that they make even attractive houses look highly unattractive.

If you want to get interesting pictures of your home you will probably need to take a fresh look at it. Approach it, literally, from all angles. If it has trees and shrubbery, plan your pictures so that these things will enhance it, not detract from it. Trees will improve the picture if you take the necessary trouble to shoot them from the proper angles and in the right kind of light.

If you study the house at different times of day you will find it changes character as the sun moves around it and the shadows shift. Try taking some pictures to show this, and, since there's no need to rush your pictures, try repeating your pictures at different seasons of the year. Here again a house changes its personality, and you can get a lot of intriguing pictures showing its different facets in winter, spring, summer, fall.

Pick the season of the year, the time of day and point of view that will show your home to best advantage

Use a tripod when photographing your home. It will help you get sharply detailed, carefully composed pictures. Be certain foregrounds, backgrounds don't dominate the scene.

As you study your home at different times of the day, you will notice that, as the sun moves around and the shadows shift, your home seems to change character. Try for a series of pictures that show subtle changes.

In planning series showing all aspects of a home, include such details as patios, play areas, walks, gardens. You'll need fill-in light if a wide range of light and shadow exists. Check exposures carefully.

Interior photography poses many special problems. Use a small lens aperture to give the necessary depth of field. A wide-angle lens can make interiors look more spacious and natural. You should use a sturdy tripod.

Perspective

A great many pictures of houses look uninteresting or unnatural because of the angles used in taking them. The too-casual amateur aims his camera dead ahead, taking the front door as his bull's-eye, or if the house is a tall one he tilts his camera skyward to get everything in. In a straight-on, his picture is likely to be a prosaic snapshot showing only the middle portion of the house and, if the camera is tilted up, the building is likely to turn up in the picture looking like a wigwam. The latter type of distortion is extremely common but it can be avoided.

When a professional takes a picture of a building he uses a camera with elaborate controls that permit him to adjust his lens in relation to the film so that the converging lines that give the wigwam effect are optically corrected. But as you probably do not have such a camera, other steps are necessary. One way is to find a spot opposite your house which has some elevation so you can photograph the house without tilting your camera. Your neighbor across the street may permit you to take pictures from an upstairs window, or you may be able to get enough elevation with a stepladder. Another possibility is to use a camera with a wide-angle lens. This will simplify matters by permitting you to include enough foreground in the picture so the camera can be kept level and that any upward tilt is avoided that would spoil the picture.

Another way of correcting distortion in a print is through a slight manipulation in the darkroom. Those disturbing angles can be restored to normal merely by tilting the easel on which the picture is being projected in enlarging. What you are doing in this case is reversing the tilt that caused the distortion when you shot the picture.

As you can tell from studying the way professional photographers depict a house, there's more to it than taking a few random shots of front, side, and back. Books and magazines showing interesting houses include such details as patios, walks, gardens, drives, and such component parts as doorways, shutters, and other things that give the house character are also presented. Your series should include such detail shots, and for taking them a tripod is recommended since you are after photographs that are carefully composed and sharply defined.

Interior photography. For interior photographs a tripod is essential, not only to permit you to compose your pictures but to get them as sharp as possible even though the light may be limited. Use a very small lens aperture, f/11, f/16 or possibly even smaller, to give you the depth of field necessary to keep everything sharp in the picture, and you will probably be taking fairly long exposures as a result, so a firm support is required.

Here again if you have the use of a wide-angle lens it can make a big difference in the pictures you get. Unless your rooms are almost auditorium-sized, the normal camera lens will make them look even smaller than they are. Even in a 20-foot-long living room a normal lens will cover only a corner, while a wide-angle lens will open it up so that you can see enough of the room and the furniture in it to make it appear pretty much as the eye sees it.

A careful study of the room and its contents is necessary and this calls for a long, critical look through the view finder. At first glance everything may seem proper but a second look may show one piece of furniture converging on another in an unsightly way or you may notice that you forgot to empty the ash trays or remove a pair of slippers from in front of the sofa. However, the most important thing to watch and check is the light. This can make or break your pictures. If brilliant sunlight is pouring through the windows while the rest of the room is in shadow, your pictures are likely to be poor. In them the windows will glare like the headlights of an oncoming car while the rest of the room will resemble a coal bin.

Faced with this situation you can either wait until the sun is in a different position so the light will be more evenly distributed throughout the

A long and critical study of a room, through camera view finder, will help you determine if you've chosen the best angle of view for emphasizing the room's main point of interest, unusual features.

Father-and-son handyman projects rate high on list of good picture possibilities found in everyone's home. Capture story-telling action

When your children are singing praises about the projects you've built for them, a picture helps make the story complete

Color film is balanced for either natural or for artificial light. Mixing these two lights is tricky, when shooting color pictures indoors

If members of your family have favorite hobbies, everyone will delight in pictures showing the results of home projects

There's a business side to home photography. A file of pictures could help you to establish an insurance claim or a tax credit

The kitchen is oftentimes a natural studio for shooting pictures showing members of a family having fun together.

room or you can use supplementary lighting. If you decide on the latter, use either floodlights (keeping a careful eye on where the shadows fall) or turn on all the lights in the room, possibly building up the light by using bulbs of higher wattage than usual. Flash can of course be used but it is difficult for the amateur to do more than guess as to what he is likely to get in the way of light and shadow.

Color film—a special case. A special problem is posed if you are using color film which is balanced for either natural light or artificial light. If you mix the two kinds of light, as you will if you try to supplement with floodlights the outdoor light streaming into the room, your slides will be unbalanced colorwise. What you will get will depend on whether you are using indoor or outdoor film, but the results in either case will look unnatural. Rather than mix light in this way for color pictures, use one kind of light or the other. If at some time of day enough daylight enters the room to provide good over-all illumination, take advantage of it, using outdoor film. To supplement this natural light a blue flash bulb or electronic flash may be used, but do not use clear

flash bulbs or photofloods. The alternative is to take your pictures after dark and then to use artificial light and indoor film.

If you are like most people you probably have a few favorite places in your home. It may be the living room with its big fireplace; it may be the kitchen with its array of modern appliances and the counter you designed yourself, or it may be the playroom downstairs. Whatever they are take record pictures of them to show every interesting detail but be sure to show these places being used. In other words, get some people into the pictures to add interest.

A complete file of interior and exterior pictures of your home can prove to be good business. Such pictures may help you at some time in your dealings with the tax collector, and they may be able to assist you in dealings with the insurance company or even the police. As for the first, let's say you buy a house, make a lot of improvements in it and then sell it at a profit. You will of course be taxed on it but you are allowed credit for the money you spent improving it. Pictures showing the place, before and after your improvements, could clinch an argument with the income tax man regarding the extent of work done.

If your house should be burglarized, be burned, or be made to suffer some other damage, you are expected to provide some sort of evidence as to the extent of your loss. Most people shy away from the job of taking inventory of their possessions but a set of pictures showing all the rooms of your house could provide visual reminders of what they contained, and can ultimately prove a highly profitable investment.

While your home is the stellar attraction in pictures such as these, it is only a starting place for a more significant collection of photographs. Just as "no man is an island," so a man's home is only a part of a community, and pictures of your home are incomplete unless you relate them to "the big picture" of the place in which you live.

Most of us live for years in a community and don't really see it. We walk or drive by our neighbors' homes without paying very much attention to them, and we are equally casual about the stores we patronize, the schools our children attend, the churches we go to. Certainly few people bother to make a photographic record of all these things, but they are of far greater significance than most of the things we do photograph in that they represent our environment. A further reason for recording our environment on film is that it is not likely to remain static in these rapidly changing times. For example, that new road being built will certainly alter the north end of town. The old brick schoolhouse will soon be replaced by a modern, million-dollar structure. A huge shopping center is being contemplated, and there is talk of a change in the zoning regulations that will permit apartment houses in that fine old residential section across the river. In consideration of these things it might be nice to have some pictures that will someday recall your community as it used to be.

You could plan your community picture project with the idea that you might be required to move to some distant spot in a few weeks. In that case what picture memories would you want to take with you? Starting with the immediate neighborhood, you would want pictures of the homes of your good neighbors. You'd want pictures of the business district showing some of the stores you like, and you'd want to show the hospital where you had that operation, and the church you attend. In addition to these and other pictures you would want some pictures of the place where you work, showing the kind of work that is done there and showing your own office or work area and some of your fellow workers.

If your family's enjoyment of art and antiques begins at your home's entry, begin home picture sequence here also.

*A little imagination is often all that is
necessary to get appealing picture
that conveys warmth even in a cold setting*

*If you shy away from the job of making an
inventory of your home's possessions,
a picture can serve as a visual reminder*

*A camera gives you special
reason for discovering
your community's noteworthy
buildings, historic sites*

When photographing items of unusual
artistic design, use them as a means
for experimenting with picture composition

By combining items of contrasting
design or pattern, in filming
works of art, you can strengthen
picture's over-all impact

Filming the how-to
of a sculptor's
art adds increased
appreciation,
admiration for
a finished project

Simplicity of picture subjects'
designs is enhanced by
interplay of lights and shadows

People are important. If you undertake a project such as this, be sure to include people in your pictures. A picture of your child's school may have some interest as a building, but it will be far more interesting if you show it with children playing in the yard, getting off the bus, or studying in class. It is one thing to take a few interior and exterior shots of your church but it is much better to get pictures which show people entering or leaving the church and the service itself.

Getting such pictures does not mean that you have to make yourself conspicuous. At school, your child's teacher will probably be glad to grant you permission to make a few quick pictures of the class in session, and a word with your clergyman will doubtless secure his approval to take some pictures from a side aisle or the choir loft. Obviously, in taking such pictures you should be careful not to distract others.

When you take pictures showing your job the human element is equally important. Even the busiest of jobs permit breaks when you should have no trouble taking a few pictures, but don't let your colleagues make a joke out of the proceedings. A few comical pictures won't be amiss, but that is not the kind you want for the record.

And don't leave yourself out of this series. Give your camera to an associate and ask him to snap a few pictures showing you on the job.

In all likelihood you and your family participate in community activities that are important enough to include in your picture story. Make a point to take some pictures at your next meeting.

There is hardly a community that does not pride itself on something that goes on there, that took place in the past, or is projected for the future. The town may have been the scene of a famous battle in the Revolutionary War, it may boast the loveliest waterfall in the state, it may be the site of the world's largest furniture factory, or it may have been the birthplace of a famous statesman. If so, the particulars should be part of your pictorial record.

It may be, too, that your community features something unique in the way of celebrations. If a famous battle was fought in the vicinity the occasion may be marked by special ceremonies. Or there may be special celebrations held in your community by national groups who mark their Old World customs and holidays. If so, you can look forward to a photographic treat. A Welsh *eisteddfodd* will surely provide some comely young ladies in the full skirts and tall bonnets of old Wales, not to mention some dramatic declamations and fine singing on the part of the menfolks. An Irish *feis* will give you plenty of action as the dancers do their stuff, and a German gathering may provide strenuous athletics of the *Turnverein* variety.

Quite often people living in a community are not aware of the colorful things to be seen there unless they do a little checking. With a camera you have a special reason for doing so. In all likelihood, when you have finished your project, you will have a better appreciation of your community than you had before, for the simple reason that you will probably find that it is a lot more interesting than you ever realized.

Photographs that show beauty, warmth of your home can be the center of attraction at your next family reunion

Color pictures of brilliantly hued, prized flower arrangements often convey feeling of fine paintings. Long after flowers are gone, picture provides cherished memories.

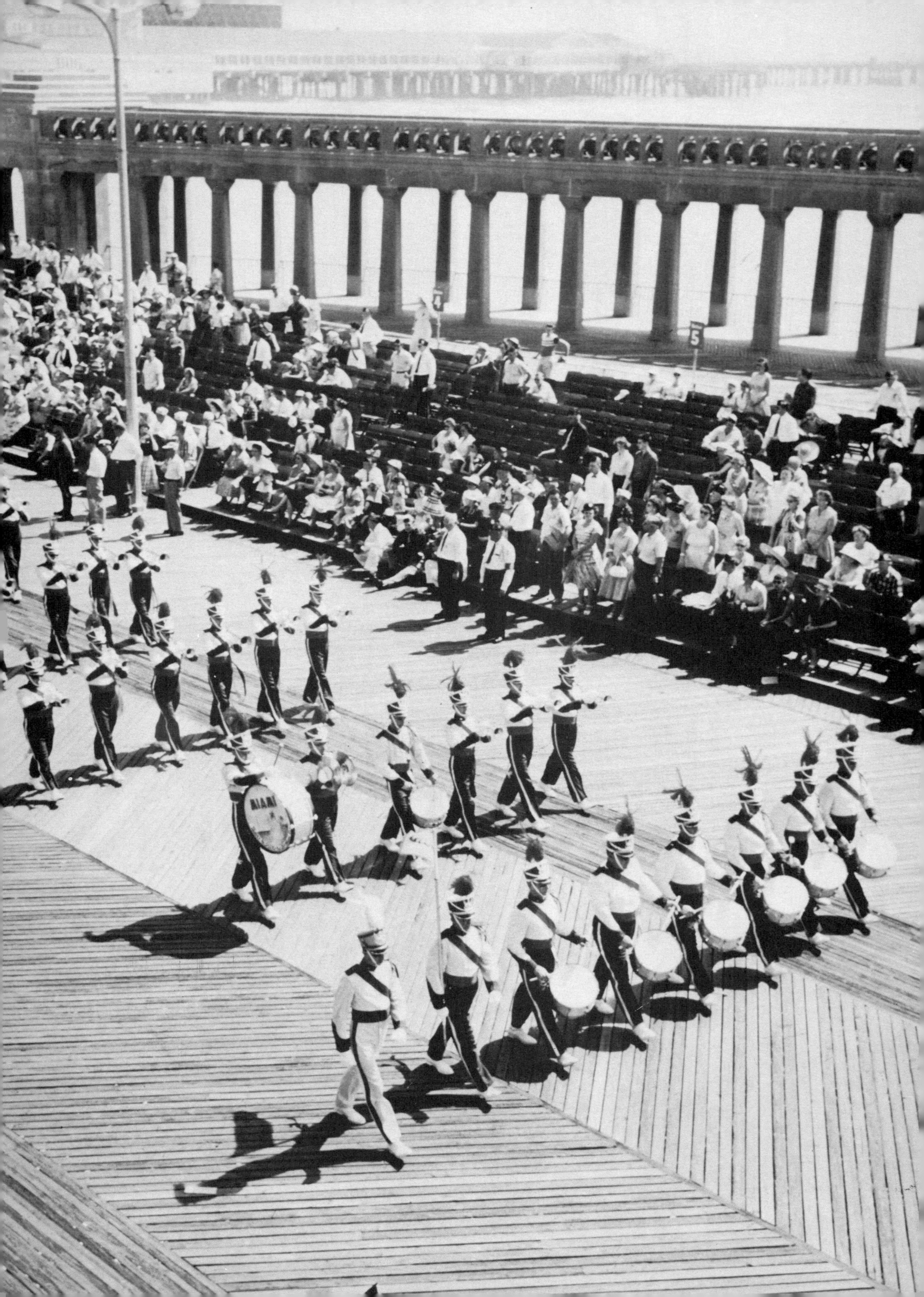
4
5

Sports and spectacles

You go to the season's big game—football, baseball, basketball. You watch a big parade swing by. You go to the Mardi Gras in New Orleans or the Tournament of Roses in Pasadena. You attend a Boy Scout jamboree or a Kiwanis convention. You take a lot of pictures.

Your pictures portray faithfully the many exciting things you saw. As they are in color, they are all the more realistic. Looking at your slides and prints you experience again the excitement of those two football teams clashing on the field, and the thrill of the passing parade; you can hear again the cheers, the blare of bands, and the rhythm of marching feet.

However, the probability is that your pictures could have been improved if you had done things a bit differently. In the course of getting better pictures you probably would have enjoyed the spectacles a lot more than you did.

It is reasonable that you will not get photographs showing close-up detail of a big sports event or any other spectacle if you have to shoot your pictures from the last row of seats in a huge stadium unless you have a camera with a powerful telephoto lens. Nor will you be likely to get striking pictures of a parade if you are jammed along the curb in a spot where you can see only the tops of the flags going by. While this may seem perfectly obvious, miles of film are wasted by people who try to take their pictures under such handicaps.

Equally obvious is the answer to the problem—pick a better location. Granted, in some cases this can be difficult. Ringside seats at a championship prize fight will certainly give you an advantage in picture-taking, but the cost is likely to be prohibitive for most people. Getting tickets on the 40-yard line for the Army-Navy football game will certainly be extremely difficult, apart from the money involved. In such cases, camera-minded spectators will do the best they can with the locations they can get, but the average person has little opportunity to take pictures at events of that kind. The problem for most people is how to get good pictures of school or college sports events, or at some near-by parade or pageant which is not likely to be as well attended as the Mummers' Parade or a Shriners' Convention.

When taking parade pictures, try to plan ahead to make sure you have the best vantage point

For most amateur sports photography, a spot along the side lines is best. If you're going to shoot from high up in the stands, or are fortunate enough to get in the press box, you will need telephoto or zoom lenses for close-up shots of action.

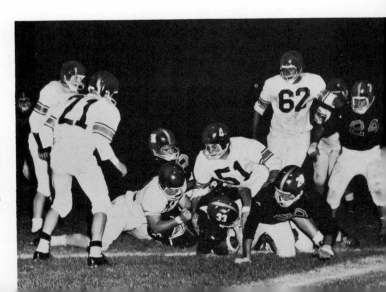

If you have any choice in the matter, there are two locations that are likely to produce the best vantage point for pictures. As might be expected these are where you will find the most experienced photographers, professional and amateur. One is at ground level, along the side lines, where it is possible to shoot action without having a lot of spectators in front of you. The other is at a height where you can look down on the action, a location such as the press photographers' box located high up in a stadium.

In the case of sports the more important the event the less chance there is of getting on the side lines of the playing field. Still, sometimes you can arrange to do so if you do a little checking beforehand with game officials or publicity people. In some cases a promise of some of the pictures you take will gain permission. If you are allowed on the side lines, remain strictly within the prescribed limits, and, above all, do not get in the way of the news photographers who are covering the game. A single offense of this sort is likely to get you escorted to the nearest gate with a request not to come back.

Following action. What you shoot from this vantage point is up to your knowledge of the game and your reactions as a photographer. If you are allowed to move about you will naturally try to follow the action. It is a good idea to get as close to it as possible. When the bat cracks against the ball, resulting in the home run that wins the game, there's no point in being at the other end of the field. Be prepared for the quick pass at a football game, and try to be within camera range to show it being thrown or caught. At a basketball game you will want to catch the crucial moment as the ball sails toward or into the hoop. In every case you can take your cues from the news photographers. They'll pick locations where they feel certain that the interesting things are likely to happen.

Sports photography cameras

For sports photography, discard that old box camera with the slow shutter; it is likely to prove too much of a handicap. You can get some pictures with such a camera but it won't do much in the way of stopping action, and once the players start moving you'll have to give up. For sports photography a good camera is a must for getting the kind of pictures you want.

What kind of camera? At one time, virtually all news photographers carried bulky press cameras taking 4 by 5 or 3¼ by 4¼-inch pictures, and many still do. The trend, today, is to carry less bulky equipment. The 2¼ by 2¼ twin lens reflex is used by many, but there is increasing use of 35-mm cameras, both range finder and reflex types. Most of these permit the use of interchangeable lenses, but the single lens reflex has the edge here because it will accept longer telephoto lenses or zoom lenses. These are important if you want to, or have to, work at a distance.

The camera should have a fast lens and a fast shutter. The former is advantageous because frequently light conditions are not good, and such a lens (of f/2 or f/1.4) speed is essential if you want to take pictures of night events under lights—harness racing, fights, baseball, football. The reason for the fast shutter, with speeds up to 1/500th or 1/1000th of a second is obvious. Sports mean action, and while it is possible to snap pictures at slower speeds by taking them at the peak of action (as when a diver stops momentarily in midair before he plunges downward) things will be easier if you can shoot at will.

The next time you plan to take parade pictures, determine before parade time the exact route, where the reviewing stand will be, and the position of the sun at the spot you've selected for your picture taking.

Some of the variables you must consider in stopping action are speed, distance of the object from you, and the angle of movement away from or toward you.

Little League ball games can offer as many chances for shooting story-telling pictures as do big league games. Try to get dramatic action of game-ending play.

Stopping action. If you are shooting from ground level, it is important that you know something about a camera's ability to stop action under different conditions. If you photograph a moving object coming toward you (a horse, a car, or a quarterback) you can stop it or him with a far slower shutter speed than if you try to snap his picture when he passes directly in front of you. Some variables must be considered, such as the angle at which the moving object approaches or moves away from you, your distance from the object, and the speed of the object. However, as a rule of thumb an oncoming car heading directly toward you may be stopped at a shutter speed of 1/100th of a second or less, whereas if you photograph the same car whizzing by directly in front of you, you may have to use shutter speeds of 1/500th or 1/1000th of a second.

Panning. You may want to use a simple trick that will make the speeding car stand out sharply against a blur, spelling out s-p-e-e-d pictorially. You can do this by what is known as panning, which merely means that you move the camera to follow the movement of the car. When you pan you can use relatively slow shutter speeds, 1/50th, 1/100th or 1/200th of a second, but when you swing the camera do so evenly and follow through with the action. Jerkiness will inevitably spoil the effect you're after.

Always remember, too, that as you work with higher shutter speeds you must compensate for the small segment of time by providing a larger camera lens opening.

Shooting from "on high." Shooting from an elevation can provide extremely effective photographs, and this is why so many TV cameramen and press photographers like to work from high spots. For one thing, the height permits the camera to look down on what is going on and follow

the action smoothly and quickly, wherever it takes place on the field. If you can equip yourself to work from an elevated spot you will find there are other advantages. You won't have to get permission to go on the field, which would probably take some persuasion on your part. Also, there's usually plenty of room and wide-open spaces topside, with little likelihood of having someone pop up in front of your camera just as you're trying to get a picture of a player going across the goal line for the winning touchdown.

Telephoto, zoom lenses. Shooting sports pictures from such a vantage point calls for equipment similar to that used by the men in the press photographers' booth. In other words, telephoto lenses or, better yet, zoom lenses. Such lenses serve to bring objects closer. How close depends on what is known as the focal length of the lens. In technical terms this means the distance from the optical center of the lens to the film when the camera is focused on infinity, but if you want to skip the technicalities you can just figure that focal length means the working length of the lens, and the longer the lens the larger the image it produces. How long a lens you will need depends entirely on how and where you plan to use it. If you want to take pictures in a big 50,000-capacity stadium, a long distance from field, you will need a telephoto lens of 200 or 300 mm for your 35-mm camera. However, if your interest lies in taking pictures of the local high school team or the Little League you can probably manage with a lens of 90 to 135 mm.

A zoom lens is one of the latest things in lenses for amateurs, although they have been used by newsreel and TV cameramen for years. This is a lens with a complicated optical design which permits you to vary the focal length smoothly. By turning a ring on the lens barrel you can go from, say, 90 mm to 135, and then to 200 mm. This means that you can keep your subject large on your film by a mere twist of the wrist. If the quarterback grabs a pass on the side lines opposite where you are sitting, you can shoot with the zoom lens set at 200 mm. If he comes straight across the field and you want to show some of the opponents preparing to tackle him, you can do this by swinging the lens to 90 mm which will give you a wider field of view.

Good telephoto lenses are not cheap, and zoom lenses are very expensive, costing $200 or $300 or more. If you can afford it and feel that either a telephoto lens or a zoom lens will justify the cost, fine. But there may be another way out, at less cost. Some photo dealers rent photographic equipment; if your local dealer does not he may

be able to help you find someone, possibly in a larger city, who does feature rentals.

Here are words of advice which will save disappointment as well as a few pennies: If you are one of many thousands in a big arena, far up in the stands, watching a sports event, an ice show, a circus or something else being staged under the lights at night—don't try to take a picture of it with flash. There just isn't enough punch in the flash bulb to carry far enough to do much good. If you have a camera with a fast or fairly fast lens, you will probably do much better if you take the picture by available light. Most big sports arenas are brilliantly lighted, and by using fast film you can chance getting good pictures in this available light.

For this kind of shooting, a lens of f/2.8 is likely to be the minimum, though you may get by with an f/3.5. With f/2 or f/1.5 or f/1.4 you should have no trouble whatsoever. Color may complicate things, as even the fastest color film is nowhere near as fast as the ultra-sensitive black and white film on the market. Still, excellent color pictures have been made on well-lit fields and in arenas, and you may succeed beyond your expectations. With fast black and white there should be no problem, but if you find yourself getting underexposed prints, speak to your photofinisher about giving your films special development. Relatively few amateurs are aware of a fact known to most professionals, that by a simple change in development procedure film can be made more sensitive.

Better parade pictures

Parade pictures are relatively easy to get. They do not pose as many problems as do sports pictures. For one thing, the photographer has more freedom of movement, but, unfortunately, most of them don't use it. They stay in one place, usually along the curb, shooting pictures from that spot from the time the first unit swings along until the last stragglers have gone by. Even some press photographers do this, though they sometimes vary the procedure by popping out in front of a unit, to snap a pretty drum majorette or a cute youngster.

Next time a parade is scheduled in your town, cover it differently. First find out exactly where the parade route is going to be, find out the location of the reviewing stand, and then scout the buildings along the way. In doing so, keep in mind the time of day that the parade is scheduled to take place, and check to determine beforehand the position of the sun at the spot along the route where you want to take your pictures.

This may sound like elaborate planning, maybe too much for such a simple thing as a parade. However, it merely means a little exercise of your powers of observation, and it will pay off in some pictures you will be proud to show to your friends.

To get really good parade pictures you will

A simple photographic trick that will make a speeding car stand out sharply against a background blur is called panning. To pan, you merely move the camera in the same direction as the action. When following this technique, you use a relatively slow shutter speed. Compensate for this by using a larger lens opening.

1. "Easy" zone for stopping car action.

2. "Possible" zone for stopping action.

want to show it from many different angles, and it is important to know about the position of the sun so you can plan to shoot with the sun shining on the fronts of the marchers, not on their backs. This is not always possible but as parades frequently wind about, you usually have an option, so exercise it where you can get the sun working for you and not against you.

The reason for checking on the reviewing stand is because this is where the most interesting action is likely to take place. Here is where "the brass" will be found, the military officials and the VIP's on hand to take the salutes of the marchers. You will want pictures of them, of course. Also, this is the spot where the special units will do their stuff, the majorettes will send their batons aloft, and the pretty girls on the floats will smile their sweetest and wave.

3. "Danger" zone for stopping action.

Table of shutter speeds to record subjects in motion			▼ $\updownarrow$	▼ $\nearrow$	▼ $\leftrightarrow$
Approximate speed of subject in miles per hour	Characteristic subjects	Distance of subject from camera	1 "easy" zone motion toward or away from camera	2 "possible" zone motion at about 45° angle to camera	3 "danger" zone motion at right angles to camera
			1 speed unit	2 speed units	4 speed units
5-10	pedestrians children boating	25 ft. 50 ft. 100 ft.	1/100-1/125 1/50-1/60 1/25-1/30	1/200-1/250 1/100-1/125 1/50-1/60	1/400-1/500 1/200-1/250 1/100-1/125
20-30	baseball motorboats diving	25 ft. 50 ft. 100 ft.	1/200-1/250 1/100-1/125 1/50-1/60	1/400-1/500 1/200-1/250 1/100-1/125	.... 1/400-1/500 1/200-1/250
60 and up	auto races airplanes trains	25 ft. 50 ft. 100 ft.	1/400-1/500 1/200-1/250 1/100-1/125	.... 1/400-1/500 1/200-1/250	.... 1/400-1/500

Work in front of the stand for a while, but don't stay there. Often a street level position is actually second rate. The reason it was suggested that you scout buildings along the way was for the purpose of locating your best vantage places, above the marchers, shooting down on them. However, this should be arranged for in advance. When you spot a location that you think will be good, make inquiries to see if you can get permission to take pictures there on parade day. Talk to the superintendent of the building or the elevator man. He will probably have some suggestions, and if it's a roof position you want he can probably authorize you to use it. Or he can direct you to the dentist, the architect, or the sales office that will be best for your purpose. I have gone through this ritual many times and have never been turned down. However, don't wait till the parade is under way before you make such arrangements. At that time, the people you will have to see may be too busy watching the parade. Or the choice spots will all be filled up.

When the marchers come along, whether you are at ground level or shooting from an elevation, be sure to photograph them head-on or from the side, not when they have gone past. Pictures of a lot of backs receding into the distance are usually pretty drab. You should vary your shots, too. Take the floats, the marching units, and the color guards with the flags. But don't overlook the human interest touches, the individual marchers who often provide humor—the small children in costumes, the clowns, the twosome on a bicycle built for two. Above all, don't aim your camera solely at people in the ranks. Some of your best pictures will be found on the side lines. That's where you will spot the youngsters pop-eyed with excitement, the lady doing her knitting as she watches, the coney vendor and his hungry customers, the men hawking balloons and souvenirs to the spectators.

Quite often when there is a parade in town, it is part of something else that is worth filming. It may be a Memorial Day service at the cemetery or the observance of some other holiday, a big convention, a political rally, or some other major function. Whatever the occasion, good picture opportunities are probably presented.

Sometimes these occasions will give you a chance to get your own pictures of nationally or internationally known figures. Big conventions and political rallies usually feature well-known personalities and it is generally easier than you think to attend the sessions where the VIP's are to speak, and get pictures of them. A personal call at the local headquarters of the organization or a phone call will let you know if outsiders are welcome—they usually are—and if they may take photographs. The logical person to ask about this is the publicity director or someone on his staff. If permission is granted, it is a good idea to get credentials, if they are available, since there is always the possibility of running into an officious doorkeeper or someone else who is enjoying a brief fling at being in charge of things.

If you are permitted to go there, your best spot for getting pictures of the celebrities will be up front, as close to the podium as you can get either facing it or off to one side. Head-on shots are likely to be obscured by microphones and a swarm of press photographers. In regard to the latter, don't get in their way. They have a job to do, and it is not made easier when a lot of amateurs elbow their way in front of them. In any case, they usually take their pictures just before the speech starts and for a moment or so afterwards. Then they retire and you can take your pictures. However, don't try to compete with the celebrity for the audience's attention by standing there taking repeated pictures. Get one or two good shots and then move out of the way.

Flash may be necessary for such occasions but excellent lighting is usually provided for important speakers, to accommodate TV cameramen and press photographers. If your exposure meter assures you that there is sufficient light, you may get better pictures without flash.

Incidentally, here again keep in mind that not all the good pictures are on the speaker's platform. Turn around and get some of the audience, and if a balcony is accessible try some from there. By covering the affair from all angles you will have something more interesting than a few pictures taken from the same spot.

Some of the best human interest parade pictures are found on sidelines or, as here, after parade is over.

Relatively slow shutter speeds may be used if you take pictures at the peak of action. Here, shutter released as majorette starts drop earthward

Chapter 6

En route

The hallmark of the tourist is his camera. You'll find the ubiquitous camera case being carried along New York's Fifth Avenue, Hollywood and Vine, Miami's Biscayne Boulevard, along the rim of the Grand Canyon, on the Boardwalk at Atlantic City, and at Kamp Karefree in the Catskills. Abroad it can be seen in Montmartre, at Windsor Castle, at St. Mark's, the Coliseum, the Acropolis, and in Red Square.

This means a certain amount of inconvenience, not only in lugging equipment and film but in stopping to snap pictures instead of just relaxing and enjoying the scenery. One non-enthusiast, deploring the ways of amateur photographers, said: "To me, it's a waste of time. Why fuss around with photography when you can buy excellent picture postcards of all these places, and color slides too?" This stand begs the question, why travel when excellent descriptions of all these places are available in books?

What the amateur photographer wants in his travel pictures is not just a certain scene, but that scene as he saw it and as he wants to remember it. This may mean a great picture or it may turn out to be inferior to a garishly colored postcard, but it's his and to him it is well worth the trouble.

What pictures should you take when you travel? Actually, those who scoff at shutterbugs taking pictures when postcards are available have a point. If you merely want a record of the countryside or some famous buildings and landmarks, maybe the canned variety of picture will suffice. But your camera permits you to portray the things *you* saw on your trip in the way *you* saw them and will want to remember them.

When you plan to travel abroad, check with your travel agent to determine regulations about the number of cameras and amount of film you are allowed to take into foreign countries. Register foreign made camera you may have when you leave the country so there won't be any question as to its status when you return.

Commercial travel pictures can never replace those you take for recording the splendor of a scenic spot exactly as you saw it and want to remember it

One way to personalize your trip is to start taking pictures at the beginning of your trip instead of waiting till you get to your destination. By doing so you will get some continuity into your photographs so they tell a story that will be far more interesting than a miscellany of pictures shot along the way.

A logical start could be made by photographing a travel folder showing where you plan to go, and a map or a globe atlas showing your route. If you go by plane, ship, train, or bus the terminal is an important part of the trip. If you drive, get a neighbor to shoot a picture of you as you start down the street. From that point on, the route can be indicated by highway signs, roadside markers, the terminals where you stop, and other points leading to your target area. If you go by ship you will obviously want to show the many interesting facets of a sea voyage.

When you arrive at your destination, whether it be a not-too-distant seashore or a remote corner of the orient, your picture-taking will begin in earnest. That is, if you keep your wits about you. Some people travel thousands of miles, lugging a camera all the way, and take few pictures. So diverted are they by the things they see and the sounds they hear that they forget the cameras slung around their necks. One man who travels a lot and who brings back some excellent photographs once explained his formula. "When I see something that looks interesting, I ask myself if the people next door or the boys at the of-

Begin your vacation pictures by showing your mode of travel. If you're going by air, take a picture at the airport showing your plane arriving. If traveling by car, photograph the road you start out on. When going by train, show the depot from which you plan to depart.

fice might like to see it too. If the answer is yes, I take it and I try to take it in such a way that when I project it on the screen the picture tells the story without requiring a lot of explanation, or excuses on my part."

People and pictures

Knowledgeable photographers do something else when they take travel pictures. They place a lot of emphasis on people since people can be as interesting as the setting. Sometimes more so. A visitor to Venice will obviously take pictures of the canals, St. Mark's and other famous sights. But these pictures can be made a lot more intriguing if you include people—Venetians as well as other visitors.

But avoid one pitfall that snares many tourists, to the later discomfort of those who have to look at their pictures. Don't put yourself and your family in all your pictures. How many times have you winced at this routine: "There we were at Buckingham Palace. That's me talking to the guard. And here's one of Linda trying to talk French to a gendarme. Here she is again on the steps of the Louvre. Here I am . . ." In short, while there is no need to cut yourself out of all the pictures, be sure to give a few other people a break.

The idea of using people in your pictures is as sound when it comes to vacation pictures taken close to home as it is for that trip abroad. A mountain stream may be deserving of photographic attention but it's a lot more interesting if you show a fisherman casting in it. And even more so if you wait around long to show him

A mountain stream may deserve photographic attention but pictures of it will be much more interesting if you include a fisherman either casting or landing a fish.

If you plan to vacation at a wilderness camp, make certain your picture album includes several scenes that thoroughly document your claim to roughing it.

An entrance gate can be starting point for series of pictures that records fun-filled day in an amusement center

Sweep of drying nets forms a natural frame— texture of nets adds to effect

Welcome a chance to include an interesting local resident in a shot. Most will pose willingly

By including people in your pictures of famous landmarks, you will gain added story-telling interest

To add variety in an album of vacation pictures, vary long shots of a scene with close-up views

landing a big fat trout. If you go in for dude ranches you will of course want to take pictures of the buildings, the swimming pool, and the horses in the corral. But don't stop there. Get some life in them, human life, by showing people riding the horses or enjoying a trailside barbecue.

There's something else you can do to make your pictures interesting. Take them from different distances. Study a professionally made movie and you will see how it shows the same scenes and the same people from different distances and different angles. The reason is simple. If all the scenes were taken from one spot, without using different lenses to provide close-ups and long shots, the film would become pretty tedious. So, either the camera is moved or "dollied" back and forth or lenses of different focal length are used to permit you, the viewer, to come up close to observe the heroine's expression, and then step back and see just what is causing her to emote in that way. This provides a change of pace that holds your interest.

You may not care to be a Hollywood pro, and you probably don't have photographic equipment to match the professional's, but you can often use this technique, even if your camera is an elementary type that cost only a few dollars. The technique consists merely in moving about. Take some long shots, but vary them with close-ups. In taking a picture of a fisherman, you could show him casting, which means a fairly long shot. Then when he hooks the fish, move in close enough to show it.

There's an old saying that "into each life some rain must fall," and this seems to apply to most vacations. Usually when this happens most people forego picture-taking. Don't you! Excellent pictures can be made when the rain is falling or just after it stops. Some photographers hope for rain, so they can get the special effects that a shower or a storm can give. You may have seen some of their work—wet streets glistening, children playing in overflowing gutters, people huddled in doorways. The big extra dividend comes from the reflections. A dry sidewalk can be a dull thing; wet, it comes to life.

This sort of photography calls for correct exposure since the light can be tricky, so use an exposure meter, and if you don't have an exposure meter "bracket" your exposure just to make sure you get what you want.

This same procedure is necessary whenever you encounter any sizable body of water. At the lake or seashore the light is probably brighter than you think. Therefore, take a meter reading and follow carefully the instructions that came with the film.

A striking effect like this does not call for a special camera. More important is the angle.

Camera checks

You can insure yourself against picture failures by making sure that your camera is working perfectly, and checking this important detail well in advance of your trip. Obviously, this is something that should be taken care of before you take any pictures but the more ambitious your travel plans the more reason for having no doubts whatever on this score.

You can learn something about the working condition of your camera by checking the various controls to see if they function properly. The shutter can be checked by trying out all speeds and, with the back of the camera open, seeing if it seems to be splitting the seconds into the proper intervals. Certainly you are not going to be able to tell if it's working at precisely 1/100th of a second, or 1/125th, but you can hear the long z-z-zing of a one-second exposure, and you can tell if the shutter clicks a bit snappier at 1/100th of a second than it does at 1/50th.

By moving the ring or level controlling the iris diaphragm you can tell if this device is opening and closing smoothly, and you don't have to be an expert to see if the film transport is feeding the film properly. With a small syringe you can blow dust out of interior corners, and you can use the same syringe to get dust off the lens surface, after which you can gently clean it with soft lens tissue. Here a word of caution is in order: Be careful how you clean any lens. It is made of relatively soft glass and scratches easily.

Whether you do this work yourself or have it done by a camera expert, the job isn't finished until you have checked out the camera by taking some pictures. Nor is it enough take the pictures; get them developed so you know how your camera is functioning—and how *you* are functioning as a photographer. If things don't seem right; if you are getting inexplicable blobs of light or if you find scratches on the film, take your camera to a dealer or repairman for a further check. The pictures you plan to make at the White House or the Taj Mahal won't be improved by such light leaks, recurring scratches, or some other defect.

Precautions with film. With your film, too, preventive steps should be taken. As an example of the importance of this, and how a simple miscalculation can have serious consequences, an inexperienced writer-photographer team once made a trip to Mexico to obtain an illustrated travel feature for a magazine. Unfortunately, the photographer made a slight mistake. He shot all his pictures in the bright Mexican sunshine with indoor color film. As a result, all his shots had a blue cast which made them worthless. This is not a rare occurrence with novices. Using indoor color film outdoors or vice versa is a frequent cause of ruined pictures. If you are taking both kinds of film, be extremely careful to use the right kind.

Mix-ups of film can often take place if you leave it in your camera for any length of time. After a few days, or even a few hours, a person may forget what kind of film he was using. Some cameras have dials which you can set to show what kind of film is in the camera, and its speed. If your camera has such a gadget, make it a practice to use it. If it does not, an easy reminder can be made with a corner of the carton the film came in. Tear off the part that tells what kind of film it is and stick it in your camera case, underneath the camera where it will be held in place. In case of doubt, refer to it to avoid spoiling any pictures that you take.

Before you get to this stage, you must decide what kind of film you are going to take with you, and this of course will depend largely on what you are likely to find in the way of subjects and shooting conditions. First of all, do you want color or black and white pictures? Are you likely to want a lot of indoor pictures, where high speed film will be essential? Or will you be taking outdoor pictures in a part of the world where the light is extremely bright and where high speed film could be a handicap?

You can, of course, take an assortment of films with you, but you'll be wise not to do so. Decide what you are likely to need, and stick to one film if possible, or two at most. And, by the way, take plenty. If you have to buy film abroad you may run into difficulties, and you may find it troublesome to locate your favorite film even in some sections of this country. You can always find film, some kind of film, but it may have different characteristics causing you to end up with disappointing pictures.

If you would like to take both color and black and white pictures it's a good idea to pick films that have the same speed rating. This will minimize guessing about exposure and if you happen to forget what kind of film is in the camera you will still know what the proper exposure should be. Or you can get by very well indeed with just one film which can be used indoors and out and which will give you black and white prints as well as color prints or color slides. This is possible with a color negative film. But one you decide on the film you intend to use try enough test shots to give you a good idea of how it works, and make the tests well in advance of your trip so you can see the results.

Water in the form of excessive humidity can play havoc with travel pictures, and if you will be traveling in humid countries preventive measures are called for. To keep film from absorbing destructive dampness pack it in moistureproof wrappings if you cannot obtain it in tropical packs. Metal foil or plastic wrappings will serve, and as soon as you have exposed the film ship it home at once for processing. The latent image on the film can deteriorate vary rapidly under hot and humid conditions.

Look for beauty in the commonplace. The crispness of black and white film lets you play on planes of light, textures of nature

Exercise imagination and a sense of good design in choosing the unusual picture angle

In a parched river bed—many places where you least expect them —you'll find dramatic pictures

*The casual passer-by often
supplies an essential
touch to a pattern shot*

*Pictures needn't all be
panoramic. This strip of
weather-beaten fence
has its own rugged beauty*

*This setting, at the foot of
a falls, combines the
beauty of misty spray and a
swirling, frothy river*

*Try to have definite focal
point in scenics, such
as the distant waterfalls,
here, for added appeal*

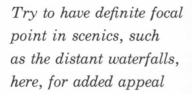

*A single figure outlined
against a wind-swept shore
reflects the solitude
found in more remote areas*

*Don't pass up pictures
of scenes you want
even though conditions
may not be ideal*

*Bracketing your exposures of
an awe-inspiring scene
helps assure that you will get
a properly exposed picture*

Taking pictures en route

Whatever your mode of travel, there are a few things to watch out for when taking pictures en route. If you go by train, plane, or bus, try to get a window seat and hope that the window will be clean and clear—not tinted. Tinted glass, used to cut glare, is not too great a handicap when you use black and white film but it distorts color film. Even so, pictures taken through glass that is tinted can remind you of the scenery as it looked to you and as you want to remember it.

Whether your vehicle is operated by a pilot, engineer, or chauffeur, you should be ready for the unexpected, which means you must keep your camera ready for instantaneous action. In a plane, focus at infinity and set the shutter speed at 1/200th of a second or faster. A haze filter is helpful for plane pictures but don't expect too much of snapshots taken from a plane. You don't often get those fine, crisp days when everything on the ground stands out as though etched, and when you are flying in a jet at 35,000 feet the ground is remote in any case.

Taking pictures from a moving vehicle on the ground presents some other problems. If you are shooting pictures straight ahead or almost so, use a shutter speed of 1/200th of a second, not so much to stop action as to minimize road movement that may be transmitted to the camera. However, if you are shooting out of the side of a fast-moving vehicle use a faster shutter speed, 1/500th of a second, to prevent blur. And watch out for poles and trees. These have an annoying way of popping up in front of your camera as you speed along.

Where you can do so, avoid shooting through glass. In addition to the problems of dirt and tint, previously mentioned, there is another handicap. Glass can cause reflections and much of the glass found in today's cars is curved, which compounds the reflection problem. The answer, where possible, is to run a side window down if you are in a car. Or better yet, stop and get out, and give

yourself time to take your pictures properly.

One other hint for en route pictures—don't take all your pictures to show outside scenes. The interior of your plane, train, bus or even car should not be ignored. Your fellow passengers and the pretty stewardesses can help round out your pictures showing how you got there. On a ship, of course, you can keep pretty busy photographing the interesting things and people you meet on board.

There is still another thing you might keep in mind, though it is hoped that there will be no reason to use this suggestion: In the event that you should be involved in an accident, try to get pictures showing what happened, who was involved, and the extent of the damage. The person in strange territory is often at a disadvantage in trying to prove his side of the story, and this is another case in which one picture can be worth not only a thousand words to you but, in addition, a lot of money.

In the interests of simplicity and efficiency, don't burden yourself with an assortment of cameras when you travel. Some people who go on trips seem to think that two or more cameras slung around one's neck are essential. One will do nicely, if you know how to use it. If you feel you should carry a spare, for emergency, there's no reason why you shouldn't do so. If your trip is going to take you abroad, check with your travel agent about regulations governing the number of cameras and the amount of film you are allowed to take into different countries. Amounts differ and regulations are sometimes vague—"a reasonable amount" is frequently cited so try to get an understanding beforehand. Be careful to register any foreign-made camera you have when you leave the country; otherwise you may have to pay duty on it when you return, on the assumption that you bought it abroad. This does not apply just to trips to remote countries. If you cross the border into Canada or Mexico, declare your foreign-made photo equipment so there will be no question about its status when you return.

Be ready to act at once when you see a good opportunity to take a dramatic aerial shot

When you're flying, set your camera's focus at infinity and the shutter speed at 1/200th of a second or faster. You'll find a haze filter a big help in taking pictures from plane.

Chapter 7

Still lifes

Leaf through any magazine, observe the illustrations carefully, particularly in the advertisements, and a surprising fact may become apparent. Most of the pictures are of a type that you have probably never attempted with your camera—still lifes. These are the attractive pictures of foods, flowers, silverware, beverages and the many other desirable things that are available for your purchase and use.

While the average amateur seldom tries his hand at this sort of photography, it is a mainstay of the professional. In any busy commercial studio you will find photographers and their staffs fussing as much over a bottle of perfume, a transistor radio, a table setting, or a can of tomato juice as a professional portrait photographer is likely to lavish on a movie star.

This is not a modern phenomenon. Go into any museum in this country or abroad and you will find the same emphasis on still lifes. Still lifes, and the museums showing them, provide an excellent starting place for any amateur who is anxious to learn how to take good pictures. By careful study of the works of masters, a person can learn what makes a good picture and the manner in which great artists solved problems of composition, color, light, shadow, and texture.

If there is no museum near you, there is certainly a library or a bookstore, and any book illustrated with masterpieces of art will teach you much that you can apply to your own photography. And as you take this do-it-yourself course in art appreciation, pay particular attention to the still lifes.

In a still life one or more objects are arranged to form an interesting pattern or composition. Lighting plays an important part in this, as you can easily demonstrate with an egg serving as a model. By moving the egg and by changing the position of the light you can take innumerable pictures of the egg and all of them will be different. When you add a second light, the effects that are possible for you to get are increased almost to the point of infinity.

Museums house some of the finest table top pictures, called dioramas. At the Naval Academy Museum in Annapolis, dioramas portray famous episodes in American naval history.

Here's all the beauty of the season captured with a harvest of fall colors. Light, shadow give life to an artistic arrangement

*Ceramic bunnies are in character
when called on to act in
a table-top woodland setting*

*Intricate detail like that found
in an Oriental arrangement
will help to enrich a still life*

*Plump, purple grapes overflowing
their earth-toned bowl make
rich picture with simple beauty*

Autumn leaves and bold masses of fall
flowers make spectacular pictures.
Choose complementary background hues

Take a fresh look in the attic for
picture treasures. Dust them,
group interesting colors, shapes

As you study your egg-and-light pictures you will get an idea of what is involved in setting up those photographs you see in the advertisements. You can give yourself a further lesson by going on to other simple objects—building blocks, pyramids, balls; each of which will teach you something more about the importance of light, shadow and texture in still-life photography.

You can, if you wish, skip all these preliminaries and start making still-life studies of more elaborate subjects, but if you ground yourself in the fundamentals, through the use of simple objects simply arranged, the more complicated still lifes will be easier to take and they will be better.

Still-life studio

Still-life photographs can be made indoors or outside, but indoors you can operate under controlled conditions so you can experiment more easily. This calls for a miniature indoor studio and a camera that is capable of taking pictures within a foot or two of the subject. You can use simple cameras—even box cameras with portrait lens attachments will serve—this is not recommended as you handicap yourself too much.

The best cameras for this precision work are press or view cameras which have ground glass viewing screens, twin lens reflexes, or single lens reflexes—all of which permit you to see the exact picture you will get, allow precise checking of the subject matter, and make it easy to work quite close to the subject.

Your studio can be a card table, but use one that is sturdy enough to support some weight without wobbling. To furnish your studio you will need some background material in the form of drawing paper in different colors and some assorted fabrics. The latter you can probably find stored somewhere up in the attic or it can be found in some closet corner.

You will need two or three floodlights with reflectors and, if you want to go all-out, a small spotlight. To round out your equipment you will need a few items for your camera. A good tripod is essential, of course, and its legs should have rubber tips so it will not slip. The tripod should also have a ball-and-socket camera support, so that you can move it in all directions. If your camera will take a flexible shutter release get one so your shutter can be tripped without jarring the camera. Since your camera will be close to bright lights, a lens shade is necessary to keep stray rays from striking your camera lens. In addition, an exposure meter is a must.

To get started with your still-life photography, using an egg as a model, you drape some drawing paper across the top of the card table, set the camera on the tripod with the lens about a foot higher than the egg, and aim the light at the set-up. But when you look through the finder of your camera you may find something pretty disturbing. Cutting midway across the picture, right behind the egg, is a sharp line. Even though you are no expert you know that this is bad composition, but what can you do about it?

This problem is common to all still-life photography, where backgrounds take on disproportionate importance. You could eliminate the distracting line by elevating the camera but that might give you an angle you don't want. You could minimize it by using a larger lens opening, thereby throwing it out of focus, but even so it would still be there. So your best bet in this case will be to eliminate it entirely by lifting that drawing paper until you get what is called a continuous background, with no dividing line at all. When you raise the paper it will be necessary to secure it to whatever is supporting it.

This however, is only one aspect of the background problem. Many times you will want to use polished wood or glass as a base or as a background. This can be effective but watch out for annoying light reflections. On the other hand, backgrounds may be used to enhance a still life. If you'd like to make a picture showing a frothy seidel of beer and a plate of bread and cheese, what could be more appropriate than a checked tablecloth as a background? Or if you want to photograph some sea shells, what could be more in keeping than a background of sand?

Although glass presents problems in reflections, you can get striking pictures of glass objects if you deal with them as professionals do. One way is to place them on a glass shelf, elevate the shelf and light them from below. Or you can light them from above. Either way, you will avoid the annoying high lights that are almost inevitable when glass objects are lighted head-on.

Another trick employed by professionals that will permit you to photograph glass, silver, or other highly reflective objects is to use a simple device aptly called a "tent." You can make one out of a breadboard or any other flat piece of wood by drilling holes at each end, inserting dowel sticks in them and wrapping cheesecloth around the perimeter. The bright object is placed in the tent, your lights are placed outside the cheesecloth, and you can either aim your camera down at the object or cut a hole in the cloth for your lens. The light is so diffused by the cheesecloth that the object shows no disturbing glare.

You can learn a lot about lighting as you experiment with still lifes, and what you learn can be applied to other branches of photography. Portrait lighting can be practiced, using as your model an inexpensive plaster bust. If your attic cannot accommodate you, any secondhand store can provide a bust that will permit you to make an intensive study of what happens when you light a face, first using your key light and then bringing in secondary lights.

The wonderful thing about still-life photography is that you need never be at a loss for subject matter. There's no coaxing of reluctant models, no repeating of shots you have taken many times before, no need to travel any distance, and no disappointments because of poor weather or lighting conditions. You have everything under control and you can let your imagination have full play.

Still-life subjects. There's a wealth of them all over the house. In the kitchen there are fruits, vegetables, glassware, utensils, and eggs. If you'd rather try the living room you'll find flowers, books, candlesticks, bric-a-brac. In the nursery the children's toy box will give you dolls, electric trains, stuffed animals, model planes. And so on through the house, room by room, closet by closet, and even drawer by drawer. Dominoes, chess men, and pipe cleaners make wonderful models for still lifes. Or you may find your subjects all set up for you in the form of plants on a window sill, a teakettle simmering on the stove, an unusual lamp, or a fine piece of china.

With such a wealth of material there's natural temptation to make elaborate still lifes; but don't. At least not till you have felt your way with the simple things. And even the simple things require study. A bouquet of flowers makes an attractive picture only to the extent that it is artistically arranged, regardless of photographic technique. Close-up pictures will bring out flaws and defects that normally are not noticed, and this is something to watch out for. A model car or an electric locomotive that looks like the real thing at the distance from which it is usually viewed may actually appear quite crude

and poorly finished when it is viewed close-up through a camera's lens.

If you are shooting still lifes in color it is essential that you keep in mind the format of your camera as you take your pictures. If you are using 35-mm film, giving you a picture that is 1 by 1½ inches, you have to think of that as a frame. Now, is the still life you have in mind a vertical or a horizontal picture? The answer will determine how you must hold your camera or secure it to the tripod. If the picture is to show a bowl of fruit it will probably require a horizontal format and the camera should be set up accordingly. If you are photographing some flowers in a tall vase a vertical format is indicated. This may require you to use a ball-and-socket tripod head to permit you to swing your camera to the necessary vertical position.

Keep in mind, too, that when you take a picture in color you have to position it properly. If you take it lopsidedly, it will be lopsided when you project it. If you are taking black and white pictures or if you plan to have color prints made, necessary adjustments can be made later. Still, it is better to be right the first time without counting on later adjustments.

Table tops

A highly intriguing branch of still life photography is called table-top photography. This uses inanimate objects to portray something or someone in real life. Serious ideas may be presented but quite often the purpose is humor. The egg that has served as an object lesson for still lifes

Set off your still-life composition with a continuous background, made from a single sheet of paper, used as a base and backdrop for your picture group.

Avoid reflections by placing glass objects on a glass shelf. Light them either from above or below.

You'll find models all around the house. Flexible figures or pipe-cleaner characters let you set the action

Fanciful gift wraps, like these pious Indian choir boys, are a ready-made picture, when set against a pine bough

Soulful Santas, chock-full of holiday treats, make an amusing reminder of Christmas fun

Capture the details of a gala party table by focusing on a single place setting—before the guests arrive

Dolls like these Western troubadors make ideal actors for your table-top photography

can be carried into table-top work, but in this role it would be given a face and a personality. One egg might be placed on a wall, a la Humpty Dumpty, and like that unfortunate character, dropped off its perch to be photographed in a thoroughly disheveled state.

Actors and props for table tops can be found in toy departments, five-and-dime store, model supply shops. Ideas for situations can be found anywhere—in real life, in cartoons or on television. Some of the finest table tops imaginable may be found in museums. They are called dioramas. The Naval Academy Museum at Annapolis has some excellent examples showing famous episodes in American naval history. The Museum of the City of New York has a number which portray facets of life in old New York.

Your table tops can be much simpler. Dolls can be your actors and if the right dolls are not available you can make amusing characters out of pipe cleaners. The same miniature houses that you use under your Christmas tree can help you set your stage, and such things as salt, sand, cotton, and crepe paper can provide the background material you need.

The important ingredient that you must contribute is imagination, and this means putting two and two together to spark an idea. You may have a figurine of a bird around the house. Possibly this china chick wears a painted look of wide-eyed surprise, or you may be able to apply such a look. With that as a starter look for something that can be made to look like a large and ferocious worm. Placed in juxtaposition, these two actors could provide an amusing photographic tableau showing what happens when a worm turns. Carry this idea further and you can keep yourself busy illustrating common sayings.

If you'd like to tackle a project of professional caliber, you could develop a table top to illustrate a phonograph record album. Some titles that you might consider are Tchaikovsky's 1812 Overture (where you could use toy soldiers and cannon), Swan Lake (starring a ballerina doll on a mirror), and the Toreador's Song from Carmen (calling for a small bull and bullfighter).

In addition to imagination and ingenuity, table-top photography calls for an understanding of composition. The pictures you take are supposed to tell a story or make a point and everything in the picture should contribute to the theme. The placement of the objects is important in this. The key object should never be placed in dead center, but off to one side, and other objects should serve to balance it. In the case of a Swan Lake setting, the little ballerina would not belong in the center of the picture but her exact position would depend on many factors —the size and shape of the mirror serving as a "lake," other figures or shapes in the picture, the kind of light and its direction, and how all these and other things are balanced.

By allowing you to move your props and your lights easily, table-top photography permits you to study the patterns that are important to an understanding of composition. In real life a group of trees may shape up as triangles or groups of triangles. A housing development seen from a height breaks up into squares, or its streets may be so laid out that it forms a series of S-curves, while moving speedboats on a lake form angular wave patterns. A chartered plane would permit you to observe these examples of composition from several hundred feet, but you can reproduce all of them in miniature on your card table studio with toy trees, miniature houses, model speedboats (plus aluminum foil for those wave patterns), and lights to assist you in emphasizing the patterns you establish.

Lights can do more than produce the illumination you need for your pictures. They can also establish a mood and even simulate different outdoor conditions. You have probably heard the expressions "high key" and "low key." The former applies to anything that is bright and fully lighted with little shadow. Painters are working in high key when they drench their pictures in light tones to express a bright, joyous mood. "Low key" uses dark tones to express a somber mood, such as an old woman in mourning, with shadows on her deeply lined face. Your table tops can be lighted accordingly. If you want to show some happy pipe-cleaner characters doing the twist, pour on the light. If you want to show a monster skulking among tombstones, you will obviously want to deal in darkness and shadows.

Light can also set your stage by helping to simulate real-life conditions. By shifting your lights you can have midday sun (permitting you to illustrate that famous Cole Porter line about "mad dogs and Englishmen," who have a preference for gadding about when the sun reaches its zenith). By shifting the light lower you can provide the long shadows that go with late afternoon. If you want to depict a haunted house you can turn off the sun and drench the scene in moonlight, using an illuminated paper moon in a dark blue paper sky.

Christmas cards

Table-top photography can produce pictures that make perfect personalized Christmas cards, particularly if you supply some imagination. Props can be simple. Even a single Christmas tree ornament will do. Get an artistic friend to letter your greeting on it, hang it on a pine bough and shoot. Or use a toy sled with Santa Claus in it. Place it on a snow-covered incline and snap it. Your message can appear in the foreground, written on a toy billboard of the type sold for model train layouts. Or get several miniature Santas, place them in a line as though they were picketing, and have them hold signs expressing your sentiments. If you'd prefer a religious-type card, simply take a picture of the nativity set you place under your tree. Write your greeting on a light space, and have it copied. In case lettering for your cards presents a problem, you can get the message across by using letters of the type available for movie titles. Or you can use children's alphabet blocks to spell out your greetings and your name.

Not long ago, photographic Christmas cards were available only in black and white. Now the price of color prints has been reduced to a point where there is no financial problem involved in having your own personalized greetings in color —all that is needed is just a bit of mental effort involving applied imagination.

In table top photography you can create your own sets and lighting effects—ideal for Christmas-card pictures.

Chapter 8

Trick photography

There are two kinds of camera tricks, one that you might call "tricks of the trade," and the other the kind that mystifies people. The former is exemplified by the judicious use of lights and retouching by the portrait photographer who wants to make his subject look attractive, and also by the amateur who holds a pine bough in front of his camera lens as a means of providing a frame for his picture.

The other kind of camera trickery is an amusing pastime that is too often neglected by amateurs. This is represented by photographs that show people minus their heads or walking up the sides of steep buildings. Such photography turns one person into two or more, places boys in bot-

tles, permits girls to swim in glasses of champagne, and otherwise portrays all sorts of zany happenings in a photographic wonderland.

What makes such trickery all the more effective are two widely held beliefs, that (a) the camera doesn't lie, and (b) a picture is worth a thousand words; presumably all true.

Some trick photographs are extremely simple, involving only a few readily available props or the ingenious use of perspective, while others call for some technical skill or special equipment. An example of the first type would show two people, one with a bow in his hand and the other with an apple on his head—with an arrow piercing it. It's the old William Tell routine, but this latter-day

A few props and a little ingenuity are often all you need to produce a trick photograph. This amusing study of a man and his dog resulted from combining two negatives in making print

It's easy to get tricky effect involving perspective. Secret behind this scene of man holding a car in the air is simple. Photographer and man are quite a distance from car. Careful alignment of subjects in view finder makes it appear that the car is being held in air on man's hand.

It is possible to convert a continuous tone image to a line drawing by photographic operations. You can do it in your own darkroom or have it done commercially

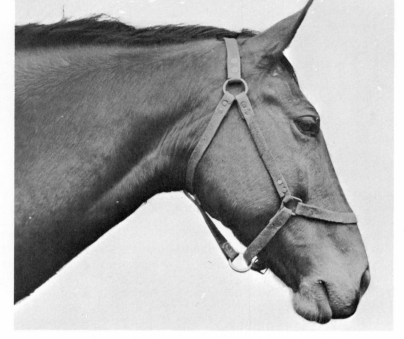

To achieve this pen-and-ink drawing effect you need special materials. The process involves combining positive and negative of same image and projecting on high contrast film

An extension tube or a bellows
attachment helps to get
awesome but amusing close-ups

← To get this silhouette effect, have all
light concentrated on background;
none on subjects. With children, use
a fast shutter speed. Take your
exposure meter reading on background

Unusual photographic effects are →
possible through use of scissors and
paste. "Father" in this father-son
study was taken from a low position,
son from a high position. Two pictures
pasted together and rephotographed

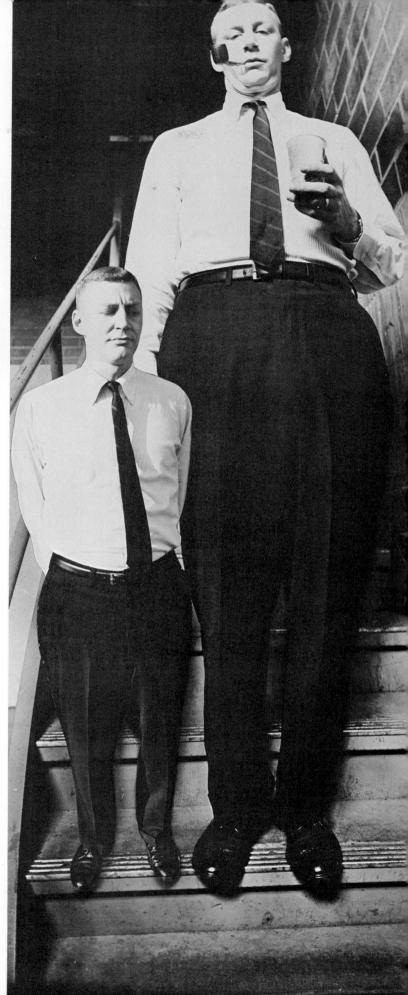

Tell was a good marksman, too, because there's the picture to prove it.

Another simple trick picture can be made with a picture frame, as large and ornate as possible. Place your subject behind the frame but add some touches to show that this is no conventional portrait. Have the subject smoking a pipe or cigar, with smoke billowing outside the confines of the frame. Or have his arm hooked around the outside of the frame. Such a picture is all the more effective if you can set the frame in a wall opening or in some other way disguise it so that it appears to be hanging flat on the wall.

Perspective

The kind of trick shot that involves perspective can be staged by two people, one fairly close to the camera and the other at a distance. The former will of course appear large and the latter will be small. The trick is to align both figures so that the distant one appears to be a doll manipulated by the person in the foreground. A common version of this shows the background figure being held, doll-like, in the palm of the hand of the person close to the camera, but this basic idea can be given many variations. For example, you could place the near figure in front of or alongside of a stand on which the small figure would be acting the part of a marionette, complete with strings. Such a stand could be easily improvised with a couple of horizontal boards, and perspective would provide the illusion of a spectator watching a puppet show.

An eye-popping kind of trick photograph can be made very simply with a single light, flash or photoflood, appropriate make-up and costuming, and a piece of dry ice. All this is guaranteed to make a person look like the very devil. A subject is made up like Satan, then a bright light is placed at a low angle in front of him, so that it is aimed upwards at this face. This will cause diabolical face shadows, and the final touch is provided by placing the dry ice in a pan just below the subject and pouring some water on it. This will cause clouds of smoke to billow up, and it will serve as an effective substitute for the sulfur-and-brimstone variety.

Double exposure

Another unearthly effect can be obtained by intentional double exposure. The end result in this case is a ghostly image, obviously pure ectoplasm because it is transparent. All you need are a black background and a tripod. The black background is important to provide the proper degree of contrast between the live person and the ghost. However, you may be able to get the right effect if you stage your picture in a dark hallway or set it up in an opening between two rooms with no light in the farther room.

To set the stage you could dress your main subject to represent a swami consulting a crystal ball. Set him before a table and photograph him in that mystic act, then keep him in the same position while the "ghost" is introduced. The camera of course must be kept in the same location, therefore the tripod. When the sheet-draped character enacting the ghost is put in place, a second exposure is then made on the same frame of film. The trick is that this second exposure is only half that of the first, so the "ghost" does not register fully on the film and appears to be transparent. To dramatize this, a prop of some sort should be placed behind him at the time the first exposure is made and it will show through the ghostly sheets in the finished picture.

If you want to depict a split personality, by turning one person into two or more, you can do so with a variation on the trick that produced the ghost picture. Here again you will need that dark background and tripod. Place your subject at a table, before a piano keyboard or wherever else the action is to take place, and take his picture. Normal exposure is used but do not advance the film. Then move the subject to a different position and repeat the procedure. For example, if you took the first picture as he was playing the piano, slide him along the bench and take the second picture at the new spot, employing the same exposure. In this case your finished picture will show the pianist playing a duet with himself, though you could show him playing cards with himself or singing a duet, trio or quartet—supplying all the voices. The secret of this trick is that the black background does not register on the film, only the figure you place in front of it. Therefore, you can make several exposures of the same person in different locations.

You can get the same doubling-up effect without using a black background by placing a piece of black cardboard or any opaque material in front of the lens so it partly obscures it. The first exposure is made with the lens partly screened with the mask, then a second exposure is made with the subject in the new position and the mask moved so it covers the other side of the lens. The advantage of this system is that all else in the picture will be normal.

If your camera does not permit double exposures, you can still take such pictures. Do it the way Daguerre and other old-timers did. Put a lens cap on the lens. When you are about ready to take the picture open the shutter and leave it open, removing and replacing the lens cap quickly each time you want to make an exposure.

It is possible to do some doubling-up with mirrors too. A simple arrangement is to place a large mirror on a table and then have your subject sit behind it so that you get two images, the normal one and one reflected down on it.

If you want to experiment with two or three mirrors you can get even more striking results.

Set up in combination, two mirrors can multiply an image so it stretches off into infinity. A model posed before such a setup will look like a veritable regiment. On one occasion a picture magazine used a three-unit dressing mirror to show attractive twin entertainers. One girl faced the camera and the other faced one of the side mirrors. The result was an unusually rounded picture of the pair that the mirrors had increased to three.

Composite pictures

Even stranger effects can be obtained by use of scissors and paste, providing what are called composite pictures. Here the idea is to match up parts of different pictures, paste them together so they seem authentic, and then re-photograph them. An example of this technique might show a person carrying the head of some poor unfortunate on a tray, in the manner made famous by Salome. To make such a picture the person would be photographed holding an empty tray, a head from another photograph would be cut out and pasted down on the tray, and the ensemble photographed. The trick is to make sure all parts of the picture are in the proper scale.

This composite photo technique has been used over the years for many purposes, some amusing, some fraudulent, but most of them quite legitimate. It was once the hallmark of a particularly lurid brand of journalism. If the newspaper couldn't get legitimate photographs it manufactured them out of stock photos, artwork, paste pot, and scissors. Photographs of this sort have turned up repeatedly in courts of law but the composite has many legitimate uses. It is often used in advertising. With it an automobile manufacturer can show a giant holding one of his cars in his hand, presumably considering its fine points. Or, conversely, with this technique a swarm of Lilliputian housewives can be depicted as they inspect a new range or refrigerator, admiring various and sundry features.

You can show yourself in a reckless role by the judicious use of paste and scissors, plus a few pictures you can take on your next trip to a mountain or rock quarry. Take a few snapshots that show the face of a rock, then have someone take a picture of devil-may-care you hanging onto a rope suspended from a tree. When you make a composite showing you working your way up that sheer cliff who can deny that you were

When combining two negatives and then projecting them as one, watch that two originals are scaled properly. The more precisely you match them, the more natural and lifelike your trick pictures will turn out to be.

scaling the Matterhorn, or Mount Everest for that matter? Or get a picture of a champion skier as he flies off into space, insert your face where his was and people will marvel at your skill.

If you have access to a darkroom or if you have a photofinisher who is willing to go along on a gag, you can get bizarre effects by combining two negatives in a sandwich and then projecting them as one. This is the procedure that is followed to show a boy in a bottle, a girl in a goldfish tank or a friend submerged in a brandy glass.

It is possible that you can find among your negatives some that can be paired off in this way, but you will get better results if you start from scratch. This will permit you to scale your pictures properly, an important detail when you are trying to fit a friend into a gallon jug. The more precise the matching job the more natural and lifelike your trick picture will turn out to be.

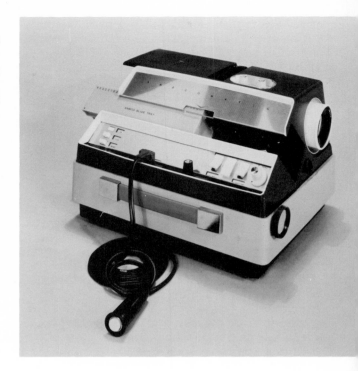

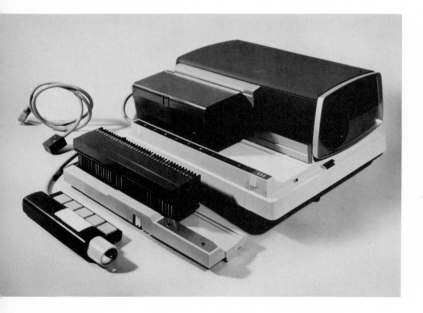

Projectors have ingenious methods of handling slides. Many have remote control, including wireless remote control. Some have provisions for synchronizing sound with the pictures. You can even get slide projectors built into consoles that have rear projection so picture looks like television screen image

Chapter 9

Picture showmanship

Not many years ago the average amateur photographer displayed his pictures quite simply by taking them from the envelope in which they came and passing them around to anyone interested in seeing them. A few amateurs, with a sense of showmanship, pasted their pictures in albums.

Today because of color photography a new approach is called for in showing the pictures you take. Approximately half of the amateur still pictures being made today are in color and the proportion is growing greater. This means there is increasing emphasis on slides and slide projection, evidence of which can be seen in any camera magazine or photo shop where slide projectors are given almost as much attention as cameras. Most projectors have ingenious methods of handling the slides; many of them are automated with such features as remote control (including wireless remote control); and some even have provisions for synchronizing sound with the pictures. Indeed, one manufacturer offers a slide projector built into a console, providing rear projection so the picture looks like the image on a television screen. The price of this unit is somewhat higher than that of most TV sets.

Still, even with such advanced equipment to help them get the most out of their pictures, there are many who exhibit their slides with such poor showmanship that hapless viewers have all they can do to stay awake.

Possibly you, too, have suffered through such performances, with an accompanying monologue running something like this:

"Now Charlie, if you'll turn off that light we'll get started. No, that's the wrong slide. There, that's better. Now, this first slide . . . Oops, upside down! Just a minute now till I figure out which end is supposed to be up. Now let me have a few seconds to focus it better. Sorry, I guess this is the one where I moved the camera when I shot the picture, but if you look carefully you can see that fellow on horseback is an Indian. We came across him up near Santa Fe." (At this point the monologue is interrupted by the photographer's wife who observes that they saw the Indian near Flagstaff *not* Santa Fe. When this point is cleared up the showing continues.)

Such showings have a way of going on interminably, to the complete and utter boredom of everyone who has to sit through them. And equally annoying is the fellow who hands you several boxes of slides and asks you to look at them by holding them up to the light, or through a peephole viewer, while he gives you a lengthy lecture on each slide.

What is the right way?

First of all, don't let anyone see your errors. Sure you make mistakes, just as all photographers do. But why let your friends get the impression that the pictures you take are for the most part underexposed, overexposed, poorly composed, out of focus and otherwise substandard? Yet what else can they think if you show them a succession of pictures with such defects? There's no rule that you have to project such slides, so hide them and put only your finest slides on display. It's a sure way of getting your friends to go away saying: "He certainly knows how to take marvelous pictures!"

It's all a matter of editing, which simply means selecting the good and discarding the bad or mediocre. When you do this you are doing exactly what the editor of a picture magazine does when he makes up an issue of his publication. He starts out with many times the number of pictures he can possibly use but by judicious selection he ends up with the cream of the crop. So, too, you should go through your slides and cull the junk ruthlessly. You don't have to throw away your inferior slides. Save them for record, or sentiment if you wish, but don't let them get mixed up with pictures that can make your friends think you are a wizard with a camera.

Work out a sequence. With your good pictures, work out a sequence. If the slides portray a trip you took, arrange them in the proper order. Certainly your audience is going to be confused if you jump all over the lot, showing scenes from here, there and elsewhere without rhyme or reason. It isn't necessary that you arrange them chronologically, though that does give your show a logical continuity. But if your trip took you across Europe, your audience may become confused if you show a picture of a London bobby, jump to the Eiffel Tower, backtrack to the Tower of London, then show bull fight in Barcelona.

You may find the job of arranging easier if you keep in mind that this won't be a silent showing, and some discussion will be necessary. In other words, you will be telling the story of your trip and the slides will be the illustrations for your words. Thus, you will be giving your audience an illustrated lecture, but never lose sight of the fact that the star of the show is not you but your pictures. Your audience didn't come to hear you make an hour-long oration, punctuated with a few pictures. Your pictures should carry the story line, and your function should be merely to supply a few words of explanation, like the titles of an old silent film.

Some experts on slide shows set down hard-and-fast rules that they say should be followed, and while some of them are more dogmatic than is necessary, you might give some thought to their recommendations. In general, they maintain that it's not good practice to have too few pictures interspersed with too many words, but it's almost as bad to rush through a lot of pictures without proper explanations. One school of thought is that your showings should average four or five pictures a minute. Some of these pictures may warrant being held on screen for longer periods while others may be rushed through, but the four or five per-minute average should be maintained, they say.

However, experts have a way of coming up with rules that are utterly inconsistent with rules laid down by other experts. Thus, the rule described in the preceding paragraph would be difficult to observe if you tried to follow a rule promulgated by other experts on slide showings, who contend that you should never show more than 20 or 25 or 50 slides at any one time. The numbers vary with different experts, but if you accept the rule of a 20-slide maximum, and combine it with the rule that pictures should be put through the projector at a rate of four or five a minute,

you will complete your entire show in five or less.

This obviously is ridiculous. If you build a good sequence of pictures and make your remarks reasonably brief and interesting you will have no trouble keeping the average audience intrigued while you show them 50 slides. And if you give them words and pictures that are really good you should be able to show as many as a hundred slides without causing an exodus. But if you go over that number you do so at your own risk. Out of earshot your guests may well say: "I thought he'd never get finished. . . ."

You will certainly encourage such a reaction if you crowd your audience into a room that is poorly ventilated, has poor seating facilities, and is so arranged that your viewers cannot get a clear view of the screen. You can prevent this sort of thing by some preliminary planning. Arrange things so there is no likelihood of having your show end up in a room so filled with smoke that the screen is obscured. Get comfortable chairs and arrange them beforehand so that everyone has a good view of the screen. And look to your equipment, making certain that it is in good working condition.

In this connection, the screen you use is as important as the projector. There are different types and the type you use can make all the difference in the world in how the audience sees your pictures. There is a matte screen which gives true colors but which lacks brilliance. Another type, called a glass bead screen, provides more brilliance but it has a narrow angle of view. If you use this kind of screen it is important that you arrange your seats so that everyone is, in effect, on the center aisle. People whose chairs are spread out to one side will see what is on the screen but the colors will appear weak and distorted. Probably the best all-around screen although the most expensive, is the lenticular type. The reflecting surface of a lenticular is such that it provides the greatest possible brilliance over a wide angle of view.

The projector you use should be fitted to the conditions under which you will employ it. Brilliance, of course, is important, but it is possible to have a projector that is overpowered. This can be detrimental since too much light can give your slides a washed-out appearance, particularly if you show them in a small room where that brilliant beam will have more impact. Conversely, insufficient wattage can make good slides seem dark and without brilliance, especially when projected onto a poor screen in a large room. The focal length of the projector lens is important too. In a small room some lenses will fill only part of the screen, though the same lenses would be perfect for showings in a large room or hall. Be sure you select the lens that is right for your particular needs. Projectors are so much a matter of what is best for you that in buying one it is wise to arrange for a trial in your home. Not only will this give you a chance to see if the projector gives you the right amount of light and the proper screen-covering ability, but it will also give you an opportunity to check on some other matters. For instance, some projectors project their light evenly while others do not. If you happen to get the latter type you are handicapped from the start, since uneven illumination means variations in the color values of your slides. Too, many projectors have inferior cooling systems, which means that the heat generated by the bulb can reach the slide and cause it to buckle or "pop," throwing it out of focus and requiring constant adjustment. Another thing to check is the noise level of the cooling fan. If it is too high it can be distracting.

These basic points are often overlooked by the prospective purchaser beguiled by automatic slide changing, remote control. Such features are all well and good, but there's a parallel with automobiles. How much pleasure are you likely to get out of an inefficient and noisy car, even if it is equipped with FM radio, air conditioning, plus several other luxury extras?

A projector that is properly engineered, with the extra advantage of automation, can make your slide showings a source of increased pleasure for your audience as well as yourself. And if you want to add a final fillip, a tape recorder will do it. This permits you to add appropriate background music or dialogue to your slides. The big advantage of preparing a sound track beforehand is that you can get the "bugs" out of your presentation before your audience shows up. There's no fumbling and stuttering as you try to recall the particulars about any slide; it's all down on the tape, rehearsed and clearly enunciated.

Certainly, it takes a little preliminary planning, and work before your audience arrives, but you will be amply repaid with a show in which you can take pride and in which your guests will take pleasure.

But what about the many pictures, both black and white and color, that are not slides? Unfortunately, all too often prints are shown in haphazard fashion, even good pictures that took a certain amount of trouble to get. The trouble is, many amateur photographers look upon their pictures as ends in themselves. Actually they should be considered means to an end, permitting others to share the pleasure you found in whatever it was you photographed.

As in the case of color slides, your first job in making up a proper showing of your prints is to discard all but the best. You are an expectional photographer indeed if all the pictures you take are worth special attention. Not even "big name" photographers look upon all their pictures as masterpieces; they are likely to discard a far higher percentage of their work than you do.

When you have chosen your best, you can do exactly what Grandpa used to do years ago—mount them in an album. However, you have an edge on the old gentleman because today's albums are far more attractive than any that were available to him. Still, if you will take an extra step you can come up with a different kind of album, one that can arouse comment.

The first step is to have your pictures enlarged, or at least the most exciting and interesting of your snapshots. To make them even better, cropping may be indicated. This means eliminating part of the entire picture. For example, if you have a good shot of some kittens but one side of the picture shows some annoying chair legs, tell the photofinisher that you want the chair legs cropped out so the kittens fill the frame. The work should not add to the cost.

With enlargements such as this you can start building a super-album. And to show your work to best advantage you might consider an album made up of plastic envelopes held together with a spiral binding. Your big pictures in such an album will be striking indeed.

Of course that is just one way of displaying prints. Another way is to frame and hang some of your best enlargements. Obviously such pictures should be attractively framed. Some amateurs use simple sandwiches of glass held together with metal frames. Others carefully mount their pictures and have them matted and framed as though they were expensive etchings or paintings. Incidentally, this is something that you can undertake as a do-it-yourself project. Materials are inexpensive and with a little care anyone can do a creditable job.

Photo murals. The most dramatic way to use photographs for home decorating purposes is in mural form. However, a photomural calls for special treatment not only in making the mural itself but in taking the necessary pictures.

Let's say you decide to make a mural of the New York City skyline from the New Jersey shore. You mount your camera firmly on a tripod, and starting at the far left you make your first picture. Then you turn the camera to the right, just far enough so your second picture will overlap the first one (to give you margin later on for matching the two photographs). The camera is once again turned to the right, again permitting some overlap, and so on until you have, in effect, "covered the waterfront." For the sake of uniformity, all the pictures should be taken at the same speed and lens opening, and it is most important that they be taken from the same location, therefore the tripod. So that there will be no variation in processing, development should be done at the same time too.

Advanced amateurs can make their own murals in their darkrooms, though it calls for large trays to handle the large sizes of enlarging paper that are necessary. The casual photographer will probably require the services of a photofinisher.

Train yourself to spot quickly the best angle for taking dramatic pictures of accidents

Chapter 10

Making money

Many people, like the fictional Walter Mitty, enjoy flights of fancy in which they lift themselves out of their humdrum world into other spheres. There they enact the roles of private eyes, astronauts, yachtsmen, reporters, and press photographers. In the latter role they busy themselves scoring "scoops" at the White House, photographing glamour girls, and covering riots and wars in far-off places.

Proof that a lot of people are anxious to enter such a dream world can be found in almost any camera magazine. There you will find such commodities as press cards being offered and membership in photographic societies being sold. In some of the advertising for equipment there is more than an implied suggestion that this camera or that one will make it possible for you, too, to get professional caliber pictures, just in case you want to make an attempt to crash the big time.

There is no doubt that a lot of expensive cameras are sold because of this. A person who would never think of buying a high-priced camera can easily rationalize doing so by selling himself the idea that with such a camera money-making opportunities will be plentiful.

The fact is, there are a lot of opportunities to make money with a camera, and the person who wants to do so really gives himself an advantage when he buys quality equipment. Opportunities, however, are not where the Walter Mittys think they are. And as for buying any of those phony press credentials—save your money. They won't be of much help when you get an urge to cover some historic event. There are more than enough qualified professionals available for those jobs, and these men and women have the best opportunities to make the most dramatic pictures because they rate the choice spots at places where something interesting is likely to happen.

Still this does not rule out the amateur completely. Some classic news photos have been made by amateurs who happened to be around when something dramatic was happening and had enough wit to take pictures of the event. One of the great news pictures of all time, showing President Kennedy being struck by an assassin's bullets, was made by a spectator who was located along the parade route. Another famous news photograph was made by a young man who had bought his camera that very day. This amateur was passing a burning hotel in a southern city when a woman jumped to her death from an upper window. The amateur snapped a picture of the unfortunate woman in mid-flight and it was reproduced around the world. Subsequently it won a Pulitzer Prize for photography.

How many times have been present when some exciting event took place, a spectacular fire or explosion, a frightful accident, a heroic rescue? If you are the type who keeps running across such things you should carry a camera with you at all times on the chance of covering interesting news breaks. If you follow this practice and come upon something that you think might make a good news photograph, shoot it from the best possible angle or angles, take several shots at different exposures, to make sure, and then get them to the nearest big newspaper without delay.

Many people seem to forget that today's news picture is likely to be of little or no value in a matter of hours. So, if you believe you have something good, don't wait to have your films developed and printed. Phone the city editor of the nearest big paper, tell him what you have and ask if he'd care to consider your film. If he wants it he'll give you the necessary instructions, and at this point it might be wise to make a tactful inquiry as to price. There's no sense in going to a lot of trouble or making a long trip if the price doesn't justify it. At the same time, don't expect to get rich with it. Unless a picture is so dramatic that it can be syndicated and sold nationally you'll do well to make more than ten or twenty dollars with it on a one-time publication basis.

Fortunately for free-lancers there are many other markets in addition to newspapers. There are many national picture magazines which use a lot of pictures and pay very well for them. However, when you submit a picture to one of these top-quality, high circulation magazines you are up against pretty tough competition. Thousands of free-lancers, professionals and amateurs alike, keep offering pictures to them, and in addition the magazines have their own staffs of photographers. All these people are competing for space, to such a point that even the staffers sometimes feel frustrated at being crowded out. This does not mean that such magazines are a lost cause, but the odds are not exactly in your favor when you send them a photographic contribution.

Whenever you send pictures to a publication there are a few unwritten rules that should be followed. If you are submitting black and white prints they should be 5 by 7 or 8 by 10 inches, and they should be printed either on glossy paper or one of the other enlarging papers designed for reproduction. If you are offering your black and whites to newspapers more contrast is usually wanted than in the case of magazines. Prints should be well protected so they won't be damaged in the mail and it's a good idea to mark "Photographs Do Not Bend" on the envelope containing them. A stamped, self-addressed envelope should be enclosed so that your pictures can be returned if they are not accepted.

Submitting color. If you are submitting color it may be wise to do some querying first. Most people take the color pictures on 35-mm film and some publications won't even consider this small size. Before risking your transparencies query the editor. This will also give you a chance to see if he is at all interested in the subject, thereby saving everyone concerned time and trouble. It might be pointed out that your chances of selling black and white are greater than they are for color. More color is being used today and more will be used in the future, but reproduction costs are so great that publications are highly selective. To make absolutely sure of getting exactly what they want, from a technical as well as an esthetic standpoint, editors usually prefer to call on professionals when they want color photographs.

With your pictures be sure to send complete particulars concerning them. This means that with a news picture you will have to tell who, when, what, where, why, and possibly how. If it is not a news picture, give as much information as possible. In some cases you may be called on to supply a signed model release, if the picture has commercial overtones or may represent an invasion of privacy.

Information needed for a picture may be written on the back of the print but don't use a sharp pen or pencil that will press through and damage the emulsion. It is much better if you type the caption material on paper and then attach it to the back of the print with rubber cement.

In view of the pessimistic reference to big magazines as markets for amateur photographs it may seem inconsistent if not downright illogical that so much has been written about preparing pictures for market. But there is no inconsistency whatsoever as the market generally is very good indeed, with opportunities all over the place. The trouble is, most people don't know about the

many publications that buy photographs. You can get some inkling of the scope of the market by spending a little time at any well-stocked magazine store. A careful study will disclose many magazines that you probably never knew existed, and if you check with your public library you will discover many more.

When you skim through these magazines you will find that most of them use photographs and some of them use many photos. Such publications do not pay high rates as a rule but the chances are likely to be much better for you to make a sale. Study some of the publications that deal with subjects that you know something about and see if you can think of some picture subjects that might interest them. However, before you go to the trouble and expense of taking any pictures, write to the editor, explain what you have in mind, and ask if he'd care to see them. Quite often editors of small publications are anxious to know about people who are available to represent them as reporters and photographers in various parts of the country. Using this approach might make you a "stringer" for one or more publications. This work won't make you rich but it will help to pay for your hobby.

No matter how good the newsstand or the library which provides your leads, it can display only a small fraction of all the publications that flow from the nation's presses. If you want to get a better idea of what is available, the reference room of your public library contains directories of newspapers and magazines. Some of these not only list magazines but break them down into classifications, citing those that cater to occupational groups, religious, and other groups.

However, even those directories don't list still another formidable aggregation of publications— house organs. You might be surprised to know how many of these there are, published by business concerns and associations of various kinds. Some of them are as well edited as many of the large general magazines.

What kind of pictures do these house organs want? The best answers can be found in the magazines themselves, but to find the magazines may take some digging. They do not appear on newsstands, but turn up in the hands of people who, for some reason, are on the publication's mailing list. Some of them you can rule out because they go in for a type of photograph that is likely to be beyond the average amateur's abilities, while others may require a technical approach to subjects that you may not understand. Many, however are likely to be logical markets for you if you can offer them something good.

Somewhere in your community there may be a priceless collection of dueling pistols, pewter tankards, hourglasses, or something else. If so, and if the collector can spin some interesing yarns about the items in his collection (and collectors invariably can) you may be sure that somewhere there is a publication that will be interested in a picture story about the collector and his treasures.

This puts you into free-lance journalism, which can be developed into a career if you have what it takes. However, it is realized that this is likely to be too formidable for most amateurs. What about the person who just wants to make a few extra dollars now and then, merely enough to to keep out of the red with his hobby? Are the pictures you take so good that people ask you for extra prints or spare slides? When you show them pictures you have taken of your children and your house do they ask you to take some pictures of *their* children and *their* houses?

If the answer is yes, you may have the necessary qualifications to go in business. But first test it. The next time anyone asks you to take some pictures for him tell him you'll be delighted to do so but then explain tactfully that you will have to make a nominal charge to cover the cost of your film, processing, and time. Some people don't mind asking for favors but lose interest rapidly if they are expected to pay for them. If your prospect loses interest you can explain it in one of two ways—he may have wanted something for nothing, or he really felt your pictures were not worth much. Maybe a little further improvement is called for in your photography. After all, everyone has a camera and your work should be superior if you expect to be paid for it.

What can you offer in the way of quality pictures? Once you are confident you know how to get better pictures of big people and little people, pets, houses, and sports and spectacles, apply some of your knowledge outside of your immediate circle of friends and see what happens. Take some pictures of the children down the street or in the next block. If they turn out well, really well, use them in a sampling campaign. You probably won't want to go around peddling them so give a few sample prints to the children or send them to the parents. In all likelihood some of the parents will ask you to make some additional prints or take some more pictures, and if your work continues to be good and you don't ask exorbitant prices, you can count on further assignments as word gets around.

A home studio

If you want to branch out in this field, and not restrict yourself to candid shots, it is a simple matter to set up a studio in your home. A spare room or even a corner of a room will serve. If it doesn't have a plain, neutral wall you can improvise a simple background by using a roll of seamless paper or plain drapes. A couple of photoflood lights in stands will provide your basic lighting, and you can add to this if the business warrants it. Such a studio will serve not only for portraits of people, but of pets—a sometimes overlooked source of revenue. In addition, you may be able to drum up some business photographing products that are locally made.

Every community, no matter how small, has organizations of some kind, and organizations are constantly holding meetings. If you live in a fairly large town or city, there's likely to be some sort of meeting going on every day. These offer a fine opportunity for the amateur photographer. If you don't belong to any organization, arrange to attend meetings of the local Rotary, Kiwanis, Lions, Elks, Moose, American Legion, Veterans of Foreign Wars, and others. Usually nonmembers are welcome. If from what you see you feel you can make good pictures at future meetings, ask for permission to do so, explaining that you'd like to make such photos available to members for a nominal charge. Since no one has to advance any money on the deal you will probably be invited to see what you can do. But here again, be reasonable in your charges. Good pictures at a high price may net you a few sales, but good pictures at a reasonable price will probably go fast and get you other bookings.

Wedding pictures. The social pages of your newspaper will provide clues to other money-making opportunities. Weddings offer obvious possibilities, but before you try this for pay, check yourself. Attend a few weddings, preferably where you are known, and do some experimenting. If the results are good, offer your services elsewhere. However, there are a few things to remember about wedding photographs. Some churches don't mind pictures being taken during the wedding service but in others the practice is frowned upon. Some churches allow pictures outside the altar rail, even flash, but not inside. To play safe, consult the clergyman who will officiate at the wedding. Ask what is permitted and what is forbidden—and abide by what he says.

Wedding photographs do not begin and end at the church, however. If you want to do it right, the proper starting place is at the home of the bride, showing her being given the final touches in preparation for the ceremony—the veil being set in place, the bouquet arranged. To continue the sequence, she should be shown with her bridesmaids, leaving for the church, and then arriving at the church.

After the service, the usual pause at the rear of the church to meet friends should be recorded, and then it's off to the reception, to snap pictures of at least the most important of the guests passing along the reception line. Following this, there's the cutting of the cake, the toast, dancing, and so on. You may find it advisable to take as many guests' pictures as possible since these may result in extra sales as the families concerned decide they'd like to have pictures of all their sisters and their cousins and their aunts. But don't forget, this will depend in large part on how good your pictures are.

All cameras have the same basic parts. Some cameras have more features than others do. Usually, the more features the camera has, the higher the cost

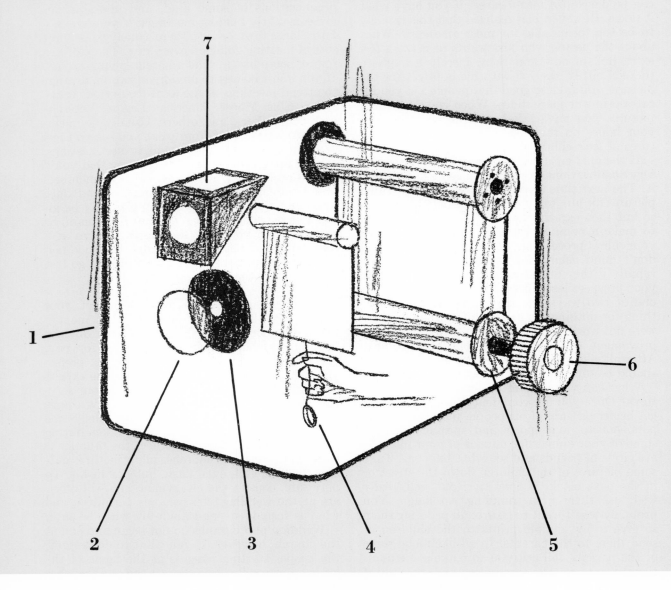

1. Light-tight Box

Keeps stray light out and serves as a frame to hold all of the other camera parts.

2. Lens

Collects the light reflecting from a subject and forms an image on the film. May be either factory-set for normal picture-taking distances, or of the focusing type, that is, adjustable for distance.

3. Lens Opening

This is the "valve" which controls the amount of light reaching the film—marked in either f- or EV numbers.

4. Shutter and Release

Controls the time that light is allowed to reach the film. It keeps light out until a picture is made. Simple cameras have a single shutter time. More versatile cameras usually have a range of shutter times or "speeds."

5. Film Holder

Holds the film in position while it is traveling through the camera.

6. Wind Knob

Advances the film for the next exposure.

7. Finder

Is used to aim the camera and show the picture area —can be either waist-level or eye-level type.

Chapter 11

A camera

A camera is essentially so simple that you could make one yourself in a matter of minutes. All you need is a light-tight box, approximately 3x4x5½ inches. In the exact center of one end make a tiny pinhole, as small as possible, and cover it with tape. The hole will serve as a lens and the tape will take the place of a shutter. A sheet of film is then inserted in the box and secured with tape to the end of the box facing the pinhole. To take a picture you place your improvised camera on a firm support, remove the tape from the opening, and give the film several minutes' exposure. You may find yourself with a surprisingly good picture.

However, taking pictures with such a contraption is doing things the hard way, and even the cheapest and simplest box cameras are not as primitive as the pinhole camera just described. All cameras have three things in common with the pinhole camera—an opening to admit rays of light, a means of holding the film, and a box where light rays pass from opening to film.

Lens. In the camera you own, whatever it is, there is a lens in place of the pinhole because a lens is incomparably more efficient as a means of admitting light and controlling it. Your camera also has a far better means of holding the film. Your camera would be primitive indeed if it did not have a means of advancing the film quickly, in addition to providing a base to hold it perfectly flat while it was being exposed. Whatever camera you have, it is far more attractive and functional than the cardboard or wooden box of a pinhole camera.

View finder. It will have some kind of view finder so you can know exactly, and not just approximately, what you are going to get on the film. Finders are so important that significant trends in photography have developed from them. The twin-lens reflex, in which one lens is used for taking the picture while a second lens shows the photographer almost exactly what the taking lens is getting, is an excellent example of this. Another is the single-lens reflex, in which the lens used for taking the picture serves as an integral part of the view-finder system. Cameras of these two types became popular primarily because they gave the photographer an easier and more precise means of seeing the picture he wanted to take.

Focus. Another function of the camera is to focus the lens so that a sharp image is formed on the film. You know what happens when you look through a telescope. The image is usually fuzzy at first but as you adjust the lens by moving the tube in and out the fuzziness goes away and everything stands out sharp and clear. This is precisely what happens when you focus your camera. In many cameras, view finders do double duty by helping the photographer to focus his picture as well as compose it. In the better reflex cameras, as the photographer adjusts the focusing ring or knob, making the picture sharp to his eye, it is automatically setting the camera so the picture on the film will be equally sharp.

This is the official Daguerre camera. The camera was made by Alphonse Giroux, Daguerre's brother-in-law.

Range finder

In another type of camera a range finder is used, coupled to the lens. When you look through the finder of such a camera you not only see what you are going to get but you can also tell by looking at a secondary image in the finder if the camera is in focus. A press camera has a ground glass back which permits a photographer to see what his lens sees, but the arrangement is too time consuming for many purposes, so press photographers supplement it with a coupled range finder plus a wire frame to show the picture area. In the simpler cameras an optical finder of some sort is employed. Such finders are, in effect, peepholes which show you a reasonable approximation of what is likely to be recorded on your film when you trip the shutter.

The lens, as the eye of your camera, is all important. However, where your own eyes adjust automatically to varying degrees of light intensity, the users of most cameras have to do the adjusting for the camera lens. (The exceptions are owners of the new automatic cameras that measure the light electronically and then make the necessary adjustments themselves.) In any case, the adjustment is made through what

is called an iris diaphragm, a series of overlapping, thin metal leaves attached to a ring, which can be opened or closed by turning a ring on the lens mount. This ring has a scale which bears such numbers as 2.8, 4, 5.6, 8, 11, etc., but while virtually everyone has used a scale such as this, some amateurs do not have a clear idea of what the numbers represent, so a few words of explanation may be in order.

At the risk of sounding repetitive, do learn how to use your range finder whatever type you have—and there are numerous well-made range finders on the market. The difference between sharpest and not-so-sharp pictures may depend on this seemingly small difference in direction.

F-numbers

The *f* preceding the numbers signifies a relationship between the lens opening and its focal length, but for the casual photographer this is not very important. What is important is an understanding of the numbers themselves and how to use them. Actually there are just two things about them that you need know, and once you understand these two things you are on your way out of the novice class.

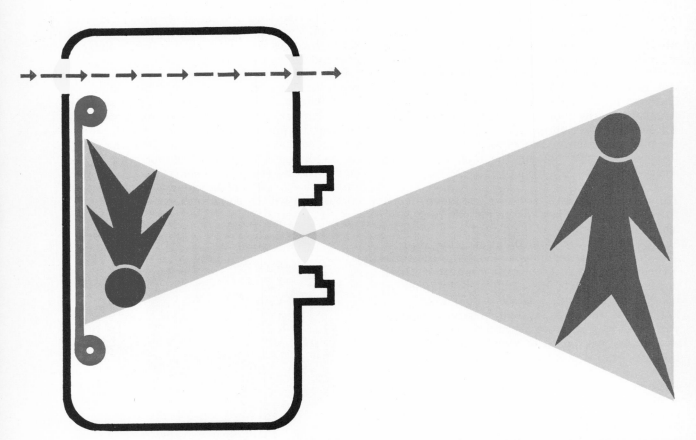

When you snap a picture with your camera, the direction of the light rays changes as the rays pass through the camera lens, to form an inverted image

Lens opening. One is that the smaller the f-number the larger is the lens opening. (Smaller numbers such as f/2 and f/2.8 represent larger openings than, say, f/8 or f/11 because the f-numbers are really denominators of the fractions— f/2.8, f/3.5, f/8, f/11.) In practice, this means that as you turn the ring to the smaller numbers you are opening the diaphragm and thus increasing the working diameter of your lens.

Amount of light. The other thing you should understand is how to determine the relative amount of light that is admitted when you go from one f-number to another. Although this seems to confuse some people the formula is pretty simple. Just square and compare. Let's say you want to find out how much more light is admitted at a setting of f/4 than at f/8. Merely square the two numbers. This will give you 16 and 64 respectively. Since 64 is four times as much as 16 it means that your f/4 aperture gives you four times as much light as the f/8 aperture does.

Camera manufacturers are now trying to spare photographers even the simple arithmetic given in the preceding paragraph. They do this by employing the f-numbers in a way that makes comparisons easy. If you have an f/2 lens the scale on your lens mount is likely to read 2, 2.8, 4, 5.6, 8, 11, 16, 22. As you go from 2 to 22, each stop provides approximately half the exposure of the preceding aperture. In practice, then, if you take a picture using an f/5.6 aperture and then decide that there should have been twice the exposure, you merely open up the lens to the next stop, f/4.

However, from the earliest days of photography it was recognized that it was not enough to provide a means of increasing or decreasing exposure by a variable aperture alone. It was also necessary to be able to turn the light on and off, and at different speeds to take care of varying conditions. So a shutter, a spring-operated device that flicks open and shut when you press the camera release, was introduced.

Shutters. There are different types of shutters but they all perform the same function of allowing the photographer to slice light rays going through the lens into tiny segments of time. The simplest cameras have a single speed while the most expensive models have shutter speeds ranging from a second to 1/1000th of a second or more plus a provision for time exposure or "bulb," the latter meaning that the shutter stays open as long as the release is held down.

The knowledgeable photographer uses his shutter and his iris diaphragm in combination. Doing so he can make his camera perform more efficiently and get certain desired effects. For example, when you take action pictures you must use fast shutter speeds, but since this means you are get-

This interior view of a Synchro-Compur shutter shows the precision construction of this intricate camera device. The shutter splits time into tiny intervals.

ting just a quick flash of light on the film from that 1/500th or 1/1000th of a second exposure, you have to compensate for it by opening up your lens—moving that pointer to one of the smaller numbers—f/4, f/2.8 etc. On the other hand, if you are taking pictures indoors without special lighting you have to compensate for the low level of light by using relatively long exposures, and as large a lens aperture as circumstances permit.

Shutters to be used for accurate color work should be adjusted, cleaned, and carefully checked by a technician for timing accuracy at least once a year. Very cold weather can hamper the accuracy of the finest shutter.

Depth of field

Here you have to be aware of something else, a manifestation of a law of optics that can help you get better pictures if you employ it properly. This concerns what is known as "depth of field," meaning the area in which objects appear sharp, both before and behind the point on which the camera is focused. Sometimes you will want as much depth of field as possible—for example in photographing a roomful of furniture you will probably want each piece to appear sharp and distinct. To get this effect, it is necessary to "stop down the lens" or close the diaphragm to a small aperture. This in turn means you have to compensate by giving the picture a long exposure.

However, there will be times when you won't want a picture that is sharp all over. If you are taking a picture of a pretty girl and there are unsightly buildings or signs in the background, you won't want to emphasize those. So, to make them fuzzy and indistinct, use the largest lens

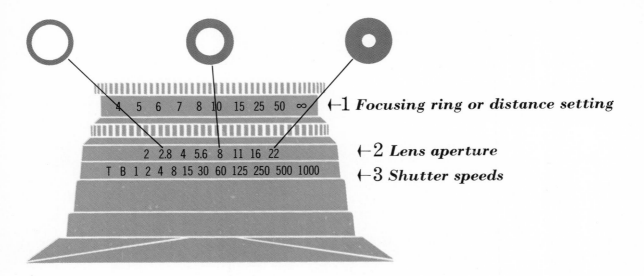

4 5 6 7 8 10 15 25 50 ∞ ←1 *Focusing ring or distance setting*

2 2.8 4 5.6 8 11 16 22 ←2 *Lens aperture*

T B 1 2 4 8 15 30 60 125 250 500 1000 ←3 *Shutter speeds*

Even though cameras of different makes and models may differ greatly in appearance and operation, all but the simplest types give the user ways and means of controlling focus, lens aperture, shutter speed. The well-coordinated grouping shown here gives a clear picture of the controls and markings associated with them. Distance setting is usually given in feet though some foreign cameras show distance in meters. Lens aperture, which puzzles some amateurs, is indicated by f-numbers. The three circles show how lens aperture is controlled by changing the diameter of the iris diaphragm. (The smaller the f-number the larger the aperture.) The shutter speeds vary, depending on the camera.

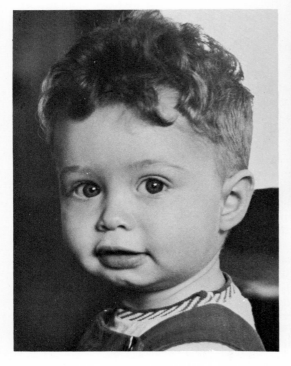

1 *Focusing ring or distance setting*

Unless your camera is a fixed-focus type it has a means of adjusting the lens so it forms a sharp image on the film. This adjustment is sometimes made manually by turning a ring or knob along a scale showing distances. In some cameras, even though the scale is shown, it need not be consulted since a mirror, prism, or coupled range finder is employed to make focusing simple and virtually foolproof. When a picture is made at considerable distance, such as the "long shot" view of the waterfall above, focusing need not be as critical as it must be when a close-up, like the one at left, is being made.

2 *Lens aperture*

When a lens is opened up its depth of field, or sharpness range, becomes less. This is demonstrated in the two pictures shown here. The one at the left was taken with an f2 lens, wide open. Focused on the bottle containing paprika, it shows that label and bottle sharply, but the sharpness falls off in the adjoining bottles, while those at the ends are indistinct. Compare this with photograph alongside. Here lens was closed down to f16, its smallest aperture. Again it was focused on center bottle, but depth of field is such that all the labels, bottles and contents show up clearly. At close distances depth of field is shallow.

3 *Shutter speeds*

Pictures by the millions have been made with cameras having a single shutter speed, but you will get superior results if your camera gives you a wide range of shutter speeds, and if you make use of these various speeds for different purposes. For example, slow speeds will help you to get adequately exposed pictures in poor light, such as that of the man lighting the cigarette. For fast action, rapid shutter speeds are essential. The football shot called for a speed of 1/500th of a second, while the smashing tennis drive required a 1/1000th of a second speed. In every case an adjustment in shutter speed calls for a compensating change in the camera lens aperture.

By using lenses of different focal lengths you can get different effects. This was made with a wide-angle lens.

The same scene made from same spot with normal lens.

Things were brought close with long-focus or telephoto lens. Lenses, on 35-mm camera, were 35, 55, 105-mm.

aperture possible, compensating for it by using a fast shutter speed.

When you do this you must focus your camera carefully. Since a wide-open lens means shallow depth of field, you obviously must be more critical in focusing than if you were using a small lens opening which would automatically provide a lot of leeway. In reflex cameras and cameras with coupled range finders, focusing is so simple that a person has to be downright careless to get an out-of-focus picture. Still, there are many cameras that must be focused manually and this means you have to be able to estimate distances with some degree of accuracy.

Estimating distances. The average person is inclined to think that he can guess distances pretty accurately, but quite often he goes wide of the mark. This is not so serious when pictures are being taken outdoors at fairly long range, since a lens' depth of field will correct for the usual errors. But because of another physical law, the closer you get to the object you are photographing the shallower is the depth of field —and this is aggravated if you have to use a large lens aperture. As an example of this, if you tried to get an indoor picture of a cat or dog, shooting head-on at a distance of two feet, using a 35-mm camera with an f/2 lens at full aperture, you could get the animal's whiskers nice and sharp if you focused on them, but the animal's ears would probably be a bit out of focus.

Picture-taking steps

In describing the component parts of a camera and their functions, no attempt was made to suggest the procedure to be followed in using them. However, it is important that a regular routine be followed every time a picture is made, since it only takes one error of omission or commission to spoil the photograph. The following is therefore recommended: (1) set the lens opening by moving the scale on the lens mount that operates the iris diaphragm, (2) check the shutter speed, (3) focus the camera, (4) take a long, careful look through the view finder, studying not just the particular person or thing you are photographing but everything else that you can see, (5) press the shutter release gently without jerking, (6) wind the film to the next frame. There may be one final point, depending on your camera. Many cameras are automatically cocked when you wind the film or advance it by turning a lever. If your camera does not have this feature, remember to cock the camera before you try to take the next picture. If you are taking a series of pictures in a short time, it's a good idea to be prepared by cocking the shutter as soon as you have wound the film to the next frame. But don't leave the shutter cocked for long periods of time since this may damage the mechanism.

The pictures at left and below demonstrate what happens when you change the aperture of your lens. At left, the diaphragm was "stopped down." Though camera was focused at ten feet note over-all sharpness.

Again the camera was focused at ten feet, but here wider lens opening was employed. Because of this, the depth of field became shallow and wooden fence shows decided fuzziness as it recedes into the background.

In each of these pictures a different focal point was used. In the first picture the camera was focused on the bench and large lens aperture was employed. Note foreground sharpness and blurred water and trees in background. In the center picture focus was on distant trees, using a large aperture. In the third picture the camera was focused at 20 feet and a smaller lens opening was employed resulting in fair over-all sharpness.

Chapter 12

Camera types

Several years ago a nationally circulated magazine published an interesting pictorial feature, showing the work of a number of outstanding photographers. The feature was impressive. But the most remarkable thing about it was that all the pictures in the feature had been taken with two old box cameras.

In the hands of most people those two cameras would not have produced comparable results, but the feature illustrates a point to keep in mind when you begin to think that maybe all your photography needs to make it professional in caliber is a shiny new camera. Obviously the person with a fine camera has an advantage. However, while a Stradivarius violin will produce superb music for a Heifetz it won't do much for a beginner.

If your pictures are not as good as you think they should be, do some honest soul-searching. The trouble may not lie in your camera but in yourself. And the answer may not be that expensive camera you wish you could afford, but a better appreciation of the one you own, and a greater understanding of its potentialities.

Even so, there are few things that intrigue photographers more than the question, "which is the best camera?" And in search of an answer they browse in camera stores, study photographic magazines, and discuss the matter at length with camera-minded friends. Unfortunately, it is a question without an answer. The nearest you can come to answering it is to determine which camera is best for you.

It would be almost impossible to describe all the different makes and models that are available. To do so would be as confusing as a walk through a large metropolitan photo shop, with hundreds or thousands of cameras on display.

This lovely study was not made

with a studio camera but

with an ancient box brownie

The wide variety of cameras available break down into a few categories.

Box camera. The simplest and least expensive of these is the box camera in its various forms. The pinhole camera is the crudest version of this. Box cameras have been the mainstay of the industry since photography was discovered. They are still the mainstay of the photo industry, but they are a far cry from what they used to be. Modern types are usually made of plastic, and they are attractive and compact. While they do not have "fast" lenses, the more sensitive film you buy today compensates in some measure for this, and many of the cameras have built-in flash to provide light where the available light might be insufficient. Possibly the most important reason why these inexpensive cameras turn in such a

Modern box cameras are a far cry from the old black box. Usually they are compact, well made of plastic.

The view camera is widely used by professionals because of its versatility, achieved through its many controls.

For years this has been traditional camera of news photographers. Ruggedly built, it too is quite versatile.

consistently good score is that their owners do not expect too much of them. The advantages of such cameras are their low cost, their sturdiness, and their ability to produce good pictures under conditions usually encountered by the average snapshooter. As against this, they set limitations on the person who wants to get better pictures. The simple lens does not permit sharp pictures under many conditions. Limited shutter speeds and aperture setting, and fixed focus make it difficult to get pictures in poor light without flash,

when fast motion is encountered, and when pictures are being taken at close distances.

Folding camera. Once extremely popular, the folding camera is now fast losing its predominant position, and few models are being made. Even so, there are millions of them in use and they do have some advantages. One is that most folding cameras provide a picture big enough so that enlarging is not required, and yet the camera is so compact that it can be carried in one's pocket. Although it is superior to the box camera, in that it is likely to have a better lens, shutter, and focusing equipment, it has certain drawbacks too. It is subject to malfunctions, in that the struts supporting the bellows are often not as rigid as they should be, and the bellows can develop light leaks. Too, the camera does not permit the use of interchangeable lenses, and view finders quite often leave much to be desired.

Press cameras—View cameras. These are alike in certain important respects and may therefore be considered together. One such respect is that neither is a camera for the novice, but is strictly for the serious amateur or the professional. Both types are highly versatile and permit the use of a wide range of lenses, and because they are used extensively by professionals, film manufacturers offer an extensive assortment of films for them. Because such cameras feature a wide variety of controls in the form of double extension bellows, adjustable lens boards and backs, they permit the photographer to correct for distortion, use lenses which take extreme close-ups (or distant scenes) and get other professional effects. Unfortunately such cameras are bulky and heavy, and the large film that they require is rather expensive for the use of most amateur photographers.

Twin lens reflex camera. One of the most popular cameras at the present time is the twin lens reflex. This has two lenses, one above the other. The lower is the lens that takes the picture, while the upper lens reflects the image up to the eye by means of a mirror. On all but the cheapest twin lens reflexes, both lenses are mounted and move in the same plane. As the user adjusts the knob that makes the image sharp to his eye, he is automatically focusing the taking lens, sharpening the image which will be recorded on the film.

Such cameras have many advantages. Their large viewer, permitting you to see exactly what you will get on the film, makes it easy to compose a picture and give ample attention to the detail that appears in it. Most twin lens cameras take pictures $2\frac{1}{4}$ by $2\frac{1}{4}$ inches, providing 12 pictures per roll of film. These pictures are large enough for viewing without enlarging and they are capable of making exceptional enlargements because of the large film area. For the same reason, transparencies of this size are remarkably effective

The twin lens reflex is popular with amateurs and professionals. A big advantage is its easy-to-use finder.

when projected, though they require a larger-than-usual projector.

There are some disadvantages, of course. Most twin lens cameras do not permit the use of interchangeable lenses, that provide wide-angle and telephoto pictures, and while you get a good view of your subject you cannot tell what you might want to know about depth of field. The picture appears as it is seen by a viewing lens, which may be a constant f/2.8, although you may have closed the aperture of the taking lens to f/8 or f/16, automatically giving you a much greater depth of field, and a different effect. For certain specialized fields, such as architectural photography, the lack of adjustments is likely to be a disadvantage, but for most picture-taking the twin lens camera is an excellent choice.

Single lens reflex camera. For several years the 35-mm single lens reflex has been gaining in popularity until it is now the most discussed, if not the most widely used, of all types. This camera, too, uses a mirror to reflect to the user's eye the image seen by the lens, and as the viewing and taking lens is one and the same, the photographer can tell exactly what he is going to get on the film. Most models use optical prisms to reflect the image from mirror to eye-level so it is not necessary to look down to see the image in the camera. The reason why the same lens can be used for viewing and taking is because the mirror springs

out of the way when the shutter is tripped. This leaves the way clear for the image to pass through to the film and on the better cameras of this type there is an instant-return arrangement which brings the mirror back to where it was at the time the release was pressed. This means there is no picture blackout. The image disappears from view for only a fraction of a second while the mirror moves out of the way in order to allow the image to reach the film.

Apart from their excellent viewing system, single lens reflexes have other important advantages to explain their popularity. Near the top of the list is their ability to use interchangeable lenses, from those of extreme wide-angle to telephoto lenses capable of filling a film frame with a clock steeple on a far hilltop. Since many manufacturers are concentrating on such cameras, with the bulk of such cameras coming from Japan, competition has resulted in all sorts of special features and accessories. That same competition has provided some surprisingly good buys in this field, not only in the cameras themselves but in lenses, and accessories. While the great majority of single lens cameras use 35-mm film, there are a few that employ roll film, and these take pictures in the $2\frac{1}{4}$ by $2\frac{1}{4}$-inch size.

Usually, the single lens reflex is considered a miniature camera in view of the fact that it uses 35-mm film. However, there are some who question this because many single lens cameras have become heftier and bulkier as extra features have been added on or built in. That seems to be hair-splitting, though, and most people consider any camera that uses 35-mm film or the small 828 size a miniature (including some that might also be placed in the folding camera class since they have bellows that fold up into a case).

The miniature camera was designed because of 35-mm film. An optical expert, Oskar Barnack, needed a camera that would make test exposures with the same kind of film he was using in his motion picture camera. The camera he developed to check his movie film became the Leica, and the advantages of such a camera soon became apparent. It might be more correct to say that the advantages of using motion picture film for still cameras soon became apparent. For one thing, those perforations permitted the film to be advanced quickly and efficiently by means of sprockets, and most important of all was the wide range of film stock that was available, because of the needs of the movie industry.

Those advantages still favor the miniature camera but there are many others. One is its compactness. Another is the economy of 35-mm film, and the fact that a large industry has come into being which specializes in processing this film for the amateur. Another is that many miniatures use interchangeable lenses, permitting great flexibility, and it is not difficult to find excellent lenses at reasonable prices. Another great

This single lens camera differs from most cameras of this type because it has a between-the-lens shutter. Most single lens reflex cameras are made with a focal plane shutter. However, this camera will also accept wide-angle and telephoto lenses, plus other camera accessories.

The lens of a single lens reflex is part of the view finder. When the image passes through the lens it is reflected up to the eye by means of a mirror and an optical prism. When camera shutter is tripped, the mirror moves out of the way.

The excellent viewing system is only one of many reasons why the single lens reflex cameras are becoming increasingly popular. Other reasons are their ability to use interchangeable lenses, and the many accessories and special features that are available.

advantage of miniatures, stems from a law of optics which means that their lenses don't have to be focused as critically as those on large cameras. However, offsetting this, such cameras and the film for them must be carefully handled. Because the film size is small, a bit of dirt in the mechanism can spoil a lot of pictures and even damage the camera. Films must be developed with precision to guard against "grain" which means a loss of sharpness and that same film must be loaded carefully into the camera or you may find that you got no pictures at all. This brings up another point: Miniature cameras can be bought for a few dollars or they can cost you hundreds. Don't buy a cheap miniature and then expect to get excellent results with it. You are dealing with a precision instrument and you will, of course, get only what you pay for.

Subminiature cameras. These have been around for many years, and while their popularity is growing, they have never had a very large following. The big advantage of such cameras is that they are extremely compact and light in weight, so they can be easily concealed and used without attracting attention. Against this advantage there are a number of disadvantages. For one thing, a fine subminiature is not cheap since its manufacture calls for ultra-precision. Nor is it economical. The film itself is not expensive but processing costs are high. More often than not the negative made with a subminiature is approximately a half-inch in its long dimension, which means that special development is essential to keep film grain size to a minimum, and every picture has to be enlarged, using precision equipment. Even with the utmost care, a 5 by 7-inch enlargement is likely to be the largest size that one can reasonably expect.

More recently, however, a new type of subminiature has appeared which offers a good compromise between the 35-mm miniature and the subminiature that uses 16-mm film or smaller. This is called a half-frame or "single-frame" miniature and it employs 35-mm film in the conventional cartridge, and gives a picture that is half the size of the usual miniature—1 inch by ¾ inch. When processed with ordinary care this size negative permits enlargements up to 11 by 14 inches, and the work can be done without special equipment. Half-frame miniatures are fairly inexpensive, film costs are halved since you get 72 pictures from the usual 36-exposure cartridge of film, and although the cameras are not as tiny as most subminiatures they are compact enough to fit quite easily into a jacket pocket.

Stereo camera. Several years ago there was a great vogue for stereo or 3-D cameras, but while the three-dimensional camera has many enthusiasts the vogue for it is waning. This type camera is designed to see things as you do, using two lenses as eyes, plus a viewing lens. With the two lenses it takes two pictures of each scene, one showing the scene as your left eye sees it and the other showing it slightly different as your right eye sees it. When these two pictures are studied in a special viewer the original scene reappears in three dimensions. Stereo pictures, especially those in color, can be excitingly lifelike. Unfortunately, they must be seen in a hand viewer for satisfactory results since the "bugs" have never been worked out of projectors so that groups may enjoy stereo slides.

Years of dependable service have proved merits of the 35-mm camera which employs coupled range finder.

Compactness and economy explain the phenomenal gain in popularity for half-frame subminiature camera.

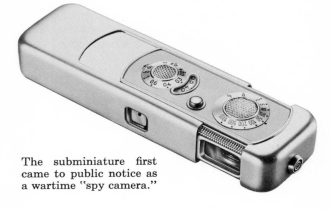

The subminiature first came to public notice as a wartime "spy camera."

Polaroid camera. Revolutionary in concept, the Polaroid camera enjoys spurts of popularity as its developers keep bringing out new inventions which intrigue photographers. The latest, and doubtless greatest, of these developments is the company's Polacolor film which permits a person to get a finished color print less than a minute after he has taken the picture.

The great advantage of the Polaroid camera is that feature of permitting you to see your picture a few seconds after taking it. When the Polaroid camera was first brought on the market it had a number of drawbacks. The cameras were bulky—

This advanced camera makes color prints in 50 seconds, has a fantastic transistorized shutter that is teamed up with an electric eye.

There's a parallel in the transmission of an automobile. When you buy a car you have your choice of conventional or automatic transmission. If you don't mind shifting gears and think that this gives you better performance you can order your car with that kind of transmission. On the other hand, if you'd prefer to save yourself that effort you buy a car with automatic transmission that will run through the gears itself. In the same way, when it comes to cameras you now have your choice of a camera whose aperture and speed you adjust yourself or you can get one that, in effect, "shifts gears" for you.

The heart of the automatic system is a built-in exposure meter which measures the light and then does something about it. One type of automatic gives a reading on a scale and the user turns a knob or dial to match this reading. While doing so he is automatically setting his camera for the right exposure. Other cameras do the whole operation automatically, actually using miniature electronic computers to figure out the best combination of aperture and lens speed for a given situation. You merely aim the camera and, faster than you could make the adjustments yourself, your aperture and shutter are set for you.

Inevitably these mechanisms will be improved still further, to make them more efficient and to cover a wider range of shutter and film speeds than at present. In any case it is advantageous to have an automatic that will operate manually, too, since there will be times when you will want to get special effects incompatible with the computer's way of doing things automatically.

most of them still are—film was relatively slow, special arrangements had to be made to get extra prints, the pictures had to be treated to prevent fading, and the quality of the pictures left much to be desired. In time these handicaps were overcome, sometimes through ingenious methods, and the Polaroid camera will undoubtedly continue to gain in popularity, though even its most ardent fans do not claim that this camera is likely to supplant all other cameras.

Automatic camera. Last but by no means least is the automatic camera. An automatic camera can be almost any of the types already mentioned —single lens reflex, twin lens reflex, miniature, Polaroid camera, even subminiature—with an extra added attraction. That is the capability of determining how much of an exposure is necessary, and permitting the user to get that exposure by a mere twist of the wrist.

A computer in this automatic ends photographic guesswork.

One of many features of this camera is easy film loading by using drop-in cartridges.

Chapter 13

Film facts

Long before Niepce and Daguerre made their first photographs, the camera had been invented. It was described by Leonardo da Vinci in notebooks he wrote in the 15th century, though he did not claim it as an invention, and a convex lens for such a camera was mentioned not long afterwards, in 1550, by Girolamo Cardano, of Milan, who said it provided a better image.

Called a camera obscura, the device was a box, a room or even a sedan chair which admitted an image through an opening or a lens and showed it, inverted, on the opposite side. This side sometimes consisted of a ground glass to permit tracing by artists who captured the projected image by means of brushes or crayons.

Tom Wedgwood, whose father Josiah was the famous potter, almost became the father of photography in 1800 when he obtained an image on a surface coated with sensitized silver salts. He was unable to fix the image and make it permanent, and he therefore lost out to Nicephore Niepce, a Frenchman, who made what he called heliographs, or sun drawings, on glass and metal.

Not long afterward another Frenchman, Louis J. M. Daguerre, made photography both practical and popular with his Daguerrotypes. These were positive pictures which had to be viewed in reflected light, the image was reversed, and each picture was an individual one from which other prints could not be made. The process which permitted the making of positive prints from a negative was developed by an Englishman, Henry Fox Talbot, and it came along a few

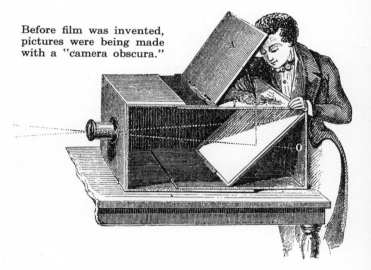

Before film was invented, pictures were being made with a "camera obscura."

You'll be able to tell quickly if you've caught charm of scene if you use camera that develops pictures in seconds

Louis J. M. Daguerre, in taking this picture, "Paris Boulevard," in 1839, made the first picture of a human being. He can be seen, in lower left, having his shoes shined.

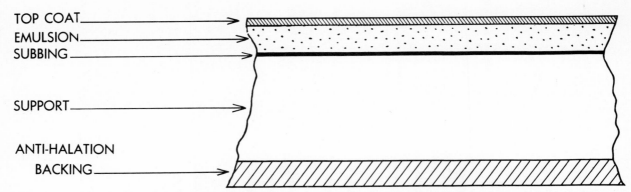

TOP COAT

EMULSION

SUBBING

SUPPORT

ANTI-HALATION

BACKING

This is a greatly enlarged cross section of a black and white film. The most important part of the film is the emulsion which contains millions of microscopic crystals of silver bromide which are very sensitive to light.

years after Louis J. M. Daguerre's invention.

In all the experimenting of these pioneers silver played an important part because a century earlier a professor at the University of Halle, in Germany, had discovered that silver could be made sensitive to sunlight. The professor, Johann Heinrich Schulze, happened to mix chalk with some nitric acid containing dissolved silver. When sunlight fell on this white mixture it turned black, but he noticed that if the material was protected from the sun no change took place. Using this compound he was able to make photographic impressions but, like Tom Wedgwood three-quarters of a century later, he was unable to make the impressions permanent.

Today light-sensitive silver salts are still the basis of photography, both black and white and color, but quite obviously tremendous advances have been made. In the days of Niepce a good exposure required eight hours, and Daguerre had to expose his plates for from 15 to 30 minutes. Today a camera that does not have shutter speeds permitting exposures of 1/500th or 1/1000th of a second is likely to handicap a photographer. Yet, just as today's camera is essentially a camera obscura with certain refinements, today's film is still basically what it was more than a century ago, a base coated with an emulsion that contains millions of tiny crystals of light-sensitive silver salts.

When you trip the shutter of your camera the light that strikes your film causes the silver to react in direct proportion to the intensity of the exposure it receives. This provides a pattern of light and dark areas, but the pattern is invisible, or latent, until it is transformed by development into a visible image. However, the process cannot be stopped at this point. The image must be fixed chemically to make a permanent picture.

That is the basic process whether the film be color or black and white. With color film, matters are more complicated because the film consists of layers of color, and processing of color film is far more complicated than black and white.

If you have ever wondered how that somber-looking color film that you put in your camera turns into the rainbow-hued slides or prints that come back from the laboratory it is necessary to think in terms of light. Basic is the fact that the colors red, green, and blue are mixed in equal proportions in the white light we know as daylight. When white sunlight strikes a bright red apple the light is absorbed, at least in part. The blue and green rays are swallowed up and the red light is reflected. The apple therefore appears red.

Color film

The color film we use has three emulsions, each of which is sensitive to a certain color but providing an infinite variety of shades. When images of all colors are registered on the film we get a picture in those natural colors. Because of these different emulsions, color film is thus a sandwich with many layers. At the bottom is an anti-halation backing that keeps light rays from scattering and blurring the image. (Black and white film has this same anti-halation backing, too, for the same reason.) Next comes the film base which serves as a flexible support for the emulsions. The next layer is an emulsion that is sensitive to blue and red. Above this is an emulsion that is sensitive to blue and green. Next comes a yellow filter layer, and the top layer is an emulsion sensitive to blue.

These three emulsions record the corresponding colors, red, green, and blue, while the yellow filter layer cuts out any blue light that gets through that top emulsion. Such screening is necessary to keep blue light from reaching the two emulsions underneath. Their function is to record green and red, and blue must be kept from them as they are also sensitive to that color.

Even more complicated is the structure of Polaroid's Polacolor film. This has 13 layers of ingredients, nine of which represent the film's negative while four of the layers are paper on which the image is printed as a color positive.

There is no need to go further into the technicalities of film and the processing of it, but it is important to know what kinds of film are available and how to select the right film for the kind of photography you want to do.

Many casual photographers have the notion that there are just two kinds of film—color and black and white—and therefore that is all they have to think about when they buy any. Actually that is only the beginning. There is a wide range of films in both black and white and color and if you know something about the many kinds that are available you can greatly improve the quality of your photography.

It is not enough to specify that you want a fast film (or a medium or slow film) because the sensitivity of the film is only one criterion. A fast or superspeed film may well be the kind of film you should not use under certain conditions since it might handicap you. When science speeded up film emulsions, permitting the cheapest little cameras of today to take pictures once possible only with the most expensive models, they made other advances, too, and one of these was to make available film with a minimum of grain. Those sensitive grains of silver in turning into photographic images sometimes had a way of forming into large clumps which cause enlargements to have a mottled or grainy appearance. The film you buy today is incomparably better than films of a few years ago in this respect, but even so grain can become a problem. There is a greater tendency to it in the superspeed films and the problem can be aggravated if the photographer or processor is careless. Overexposure can increase grain and so can overdevelopment or the use of improper developers.

Today's film is superior in still another way. That is, in its ability to record colors. Obviously today's color film is much better in this respect,

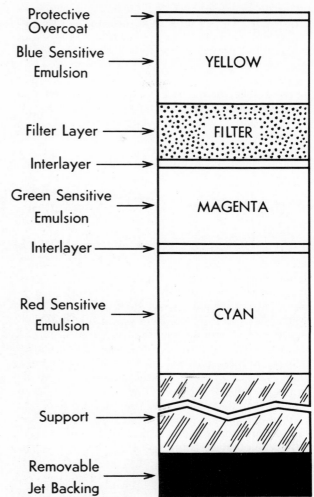

The cross section diagram of Kodachrome II film, above, shows the film's three emulsions. Each emulsion is sensitive to a certain color. The anti-halation backing keeps the light rays from scattering and blurring the image.

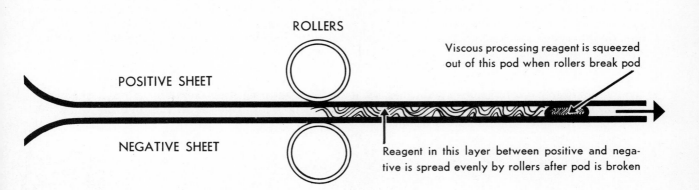

An intricate chemical process takes place in order to produce Polaroid picture-in-a-minute Polacolor print. Processing begins as film is pulled through a pair of rollers. This action breaks a pod, releasing viscous reagent in thin layer between the negative and positive.

but even black and white film has much keener vision than it once had. Such film interprets colors as different shades of gray, but modern film makes a better distinction between colors, recording them in a far wider range of tones.

Considering black and white film first, you have to take into account two things when you want to make a decision as to the best kind of film for you. What kind of camera are you using and what kind of pictures do you plan to take? If your camera makes a picture 2¼ by 2¼ inches or larger, you need not be too concerned about the graininess mentioned earlier since it won't be necessary to "blow up" the picture to any great extent. With a 35-mm camera fine grain film is desirable since the enlargements are often huge in comparison with the original negatives.

But other factors also must be considered. If you plan to take pictures under unfavorable lighting conditions a high speed film will obviously be necessary, but don't make it a practice to use such film unless a great deal of your photography requires it. A medium speed film will give you better all-around results, and if you want the utmost in print quality and can sacrifice speed to get it your best bet will be one of the slow, fine grain films. For most amateurs, though, a medium speed film is the best bet. It is sensitive enough for most of the pictures you are likely to take under poor lighting conditions, it isn't too fast for outdoor pictures in bright sunlight, and it will give you everything you are likely to want in the way of print quality.

Don't allow yourself to be confused by two terms that used to be commonly used in speaking about films—panchromatic and orthochromatic. Time was when orthochromatic films were common, and distinctions between "pan" and "ortho" had to be made. Today your chances of finding orthochromatic film are so small that there is little need to discuss it here.

Because there are so many different kinds of film on the market make it a practice to read the instruction sheet that is packed with every roll. And do this before you load the film in the camera since on reading the instruction sheet you may decide that you really should not be using that particular film at all. In any case, use the film as the manufacturer recommends, even though it is possible to take some liberties with recommended procedures because manufacturers usually build a certain amount of latitude into their film to take care of human error.

Once you find a film that gives you consistently good results, stick with it. It is significant that professionals do this and do not jump from one kind to another without good reason and without ample testing. And this goes for color film, as well as black and white.

Color films call for even greater care in their selection since there is a confusing variety of color films available to the amateur, and new types keep coming on the market. There is indoor film and outdoor color film; fast and slow; foreign and domestic; some you can process yourself and some which must be processed by laboratories. To confuse matters more you hear such terms as "color negative films" and "reversal films."

To simplify matters we will not here consider the many foreign films now being sold in this country although they are, generally, of excellent quality. Most of the color film shot by amateurs which comes back in the form of slides (though color prints may be made from them) is known as color reversal film. Kodachrome, Ektachrome, and Anscochrome are this type. These reversal films come in two types, one for outdoor use and one for indoors, although filters permit you to use same film indoors and out.

Kodacolor, Anscocolor, and Ektacolor Professional Type S are called color negative films and they give you a strangely colored negative from which you can make color slides, color prints, or black and white prints. Since such film can be used either indoors or outdoors without filters it is very versatile indeed.

When color film was first introduced it was very slow, so much so that even outdoors the light had to be pretty bright for good results. Today the speed of color film has been increased to such an extent that it is an easy matter to get excellent pictures even under poor lighting conditions, particularly if you use a camera with an f/2 or f/2.8 lens. Manufacturers are now promoting the idea of taking your camera with you when you go out at night, for after-dark snapshots along brightly lighted streets and other places where there is a lot of artificial light.

The most recent addition to the line-up of color film is Polaroid's Polacolor film. Long in the development stage, this film required some scientific breakthroughs that many people thought could not be made. Like Polaroid camera's black and white, this film comes with a pod in which is sealed a reagent jelly. When the exposed film is pulled through the rollers this jelly is spread thinly between the negative (all nine layers of it) and four layers of paper, and it triggers the processing.

Whatever color film you use, it is important to keep several things in mind. One is that color film does not have the latitude of black and white.

Whatever color film you use, if you use an exposure meter, follow carefully the exposure it specifies. If your camera is automatic, set it at the correct ASA number

Chapter 14

Light

Light is radiant energy, one of a large group of energy types which include cosmic rays at one end of the radiation spectrum and waves used in radio broadcasting at the other end of the scale. A camera in a sense resembles a radio receiver, capable of capturing and reproducing light rays just as a radio set picks up and utilizes waves further along in the radiation spectrum.

Since earliest times man has been aware that light from the sun darkened the complexion, even though he knew nothing about light's action on the pigmentation of the human skin. In 1725 a German professor discovered that sunlight blackened silver salts and since then others have carried on to give us photography. All have employed the same basic principle of getting an image by having light fall on a sensitized surface.

Few people are foolish enough to look at such light sources as the sun, a 1000-watt lamp, or a flash bulb being fired. What we are interested in is that same light reflected or deflected from objects or absorbed by them, because the extent to which light is reflected, absorbed or affected by the objects it strikes, determines the objects' visibility and type of visibility in the way of colors.

A piece of black wool absorbs most of the light leaving very little to be reflected to your eyes or the lens of your camera. A shiny white card will absorb only a tiny bit of light, reflecting back most of the light that strikes it. Between these extremes, different objects absorb different parts of the solar spectrum, reflecting what we see as colors. Leaves absorb all but the green light of the spectrum, reflecting the green to our eyes or our film; a banana absorbs all but the yellow.

Your camera is a machine capable of controlling light. Light can be bent when it goes through glass and the glass lens of your camera serves to bend the light rays to form an image on the film. The amount of light that is allowed to strike the film is governed by the iris diaphragm which changes the diameter of the light beam, and the shutter which slices the time interval into the fraction of a second you want.

As long as your camera is kept in proper adjustment it will measure precisely the amount of light you want to pour on the film. However, there is a tremendous variation in light, both in kind and in quality, as well as in quantity, and this you must understand if you are to use your camera properly. The problem can become pretty complicated, similar to the problem an oil painter

Sunlight streaming through venetian blind created this striking picture emphasizing effects possible with use of black and white film

It may take a lot of experimenting with time exposures before you achieve exactly the precise effect you're after in a night shot but the results are most rewarding.

Light changes constantly throughout day and takes on different qualities

Color pictures taken early in the morning show a bluish cast while those taken in the afternoon will show a reddish cast. If you take pictures at high altitudes, you will encounter different lighting conditions from those that you will meet when you are taking pictures close to sea level

The scene, above, taken before dawn is illuminated only by blue skylight.

A little later, reddish sunlight appears. Foreground still illuminated by blue skylight.

Later in the day, scene gets strong side lighting.

Still later, back lighting has emphasized distant haze and lent an atmospheric quality.

After sunset, the color quality of the light has undergone still another change.

would encounter if, every time he started to paint a picture, he found his oils shaded differently from what they were the last time he used them.

Everyone knows that too much light overexposes a picture so that color slides have a washed-out look while black and white negatives are dark and the resulting prints very light. On the other hand, if you don't give your film enough light it means you get slides that are dark, while negatives of your black and white pictures are almost transparent and the prints dark.

These errors of exposure are less common than they used to be, thanks in large part to the use of meters which measure the exact amount of light that is available. However, an exposure meter measures only the *amount* of light; it tells nothing about the kind of light, and light comes in infinite variety.

There are two basic types of light; natural and artificial. These in turn break down into various subdivisions. Natural light is the kind that emanates from the sun, but the kind of light you get on a bright, cloudless day is far different from the light you encounter on a hazy day. And that in turn is not the same as the light that comes from a sky dark with clouds, or the light you find in fog or mist. Nor is this just a matter of the amount of light since quite often a bright hazy day or even a foggy day will provide more actual light than will some days when the sun is out.

Light changes constantly throughout the day, too, taking on different qualities. You have probably noticed this in some of your color pictures. Those taken early in the morning show a bluish cast while afternoon pictures show red.

If you'd like to try an interesting experiment, take a series of color pictures of the same subject at different times during the day. If you wish to see other characteristics of natural light take some pictures indoors with reflected light from windows or skylights. To carry your experiment further, repeat your first series of outdoor pictures on other days, not neglecting rainy days and days that are heavily overcast. It's still natural light you are dealing with but you'll find yourself getting different effects, some of which may be far more interesting than those obtained with brilliant sunlight.

Artificial light also comes in infinite variety. Some of it closely resembles natural light but for the most part it is quite different. As an indication of this the color film you buy comes in two types, one for daylight and one for artificial light. Use one for the other and your pictures are usually worthless. There are other differences that the casual photographer does not realize but which professionals do. The kind of light that emanates from a 50-watt incandescent bulb is different from that you get from a photoflood, and that in turn is different from the beam of an arc light. And fluorescent lights run an extensive gamut.

Because of this, the professional taking color pictures under artificial lights has to take readings with a special meter that tells exactly what part of the spectrum he is dealing with. These readings are expressed as "color temperature." If someday you move into the ranks of the more serious amateurs or professionals you will have to understand this and learn how to use various types of filters in combination with lights and film to get the best possible results. The indoor color film you buy will give good results under any artificial light you are likely to encounter.

Flash light. In a somewhat different category of artificial light is "flash," which can be produced either by flash bulbs or electronically, the latter type being referred to as speed light, strobe, or electronic flash. Everyone is familiar with flash bulbs, which are small glass containers filled with a metallic filament that flares brilliantly when ignited by electric batteries. They are inexpensive and dependable (if used in a good flash gun with fresh batteries), and they are so small that transporting them is no problem. With them the photographer can get pictures in poor light, stop action, and help reduce contrast in pictures that are taken outdoors in bright light.

However, electronic flash is rapidly coming to the fore as prices of the units are gradually lowered and as the units become smaller and more efficient. Everyone has seen electronic flash being used and many photographers have used this kind of light. But such units are more complicated than they appear. The simplest, which operates on 110-volt house current, consists of a transformer, a resistor, a capacitor, and a flash tube. The transformer steps up the 110 volts to 500 volts or more, the rectifier changes it from alternating to direct current, this current is then sent to the capacitor where the energy is stored until needed. When you press the synchronized shutter release the energy pours into the gas-filled flash tube, providing a flash of 1/500th of a second or less. Such units are dependable but they must be used near a 110-volt outlet.

Another type of electronic flash uses a high-voltage battery as its power supply. This type is relatively simple, it is dependable, it recycles quickly (meaning that you don't have a long wait while the capacitor becomes charged) and it provides a lot of light.

The type of electronic flash most widely used by amateurs is a transistorized unit that employs flashlight cells. The transistor converts the direct current of the flashlight batteries to alternating current, a transformer boosts the voltage to 500, a rectifier changes this back to direct current, and a capacitor stores it until it is discharged. A more complicated version has what is called a monitor cutoff switch which shuts off the current when the capacitor is charged, minimizing battery drain.

Whichever type of flash you use, keep in mind that this kind of light can be tricky. It carries a lot of punch, making for strong contrasts. There-fore, if you are not careful you may "burn up" part of your picture through overexposure while other parts of the picture will be underexposed. This sort of thing frequently happens when in-door pictures are made of an individual or a group. The center of the picture will get plenty of exposure, possibly too much resulting in a hot spot, while the surrounding area will be dark.

One way you can correct this is by the use of a secondary light synchronized with the main light, but there is an easier way. You can use either bare-bulb light or bounce light. The former is ob-tained quite simply by removing the reflector from your flash gun, so that the light spreads in all directions. Bounce light is obtained by aiming your flash at the ceiling or a near-by wall instead of at the subject.

Wet streets and pavement will give you interesting picture possibilities by reflecting light in unusual patterns.

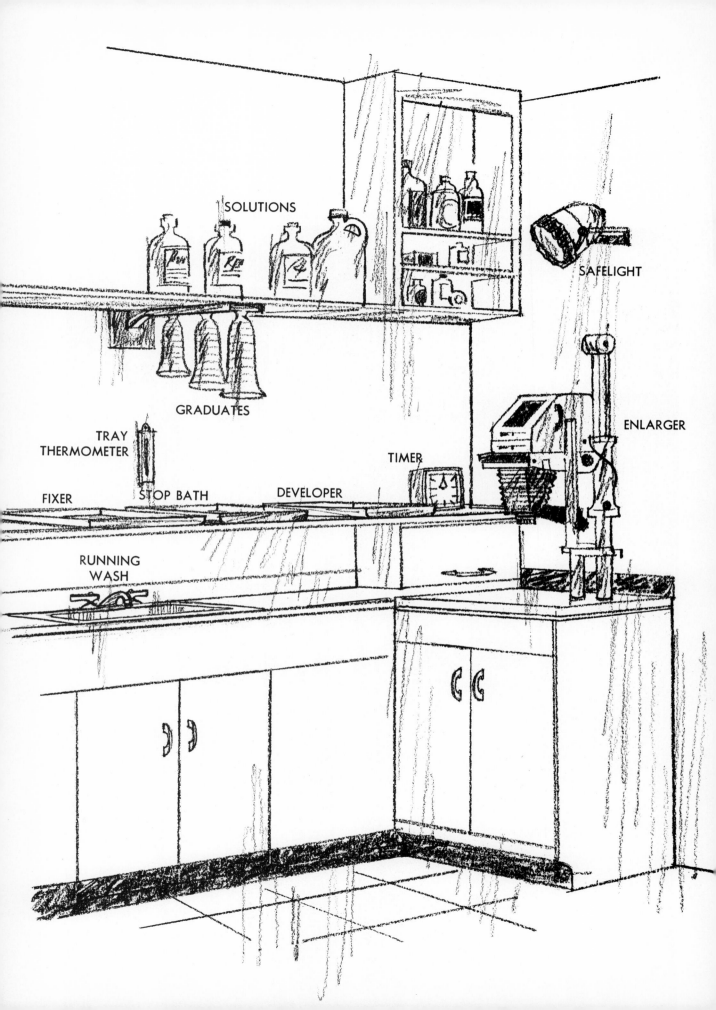

SOLUTIONS

SAFELIGHT

GRADUATES

TRAY
THERMOMETER

TIMER

ENLARGER

FIXER

STOP BATH

DEVELOPER

RUNNING
WASH

Chapter 15

The darkroom

To the serious amateur or the professional, a darkroom is an important place. Here he performs the magic that turns invisible images into things that people can see, and here he uses his skill in continuing efforts to produce works of art out of pieces of film that in themselves may be mediocre. The average person, on the other hand, prefers to leave his exposed films at a store, picking up the finished pictures a day or two later.

The atmosphere of a well-equipped darkroom can appear bizarre—the shadowy semidarkness is reason enough for that. However, you might well consider investing five or ten dollars in a different kind of darkroom, one that you can store in a closet corner. The reason for doing this is that from a nominal investment you can not only improve your pictures and get pictures that otherwise might be difficult to obtain, but learn some facts about photography that would otherwise escape you.

First of all, there's no need for a darkroom as such. A light-tight closet large enough to turn around in will serve the purposes, and if it leaks light you can always use it after dark. The purpose of this place is to permit you to transfer the black and white film from the cartridge or roll onto a reel for developing. That little chore should take only a couple of minutes after which you can do the rest of the work in broad daylight or in room light.

That work is simplicity itself. You simply pour some developing solution into the light-tight tank and give it an occasional gentle rock during the prescribed time of development. Then pour the solution out, run some water into the tank for a minute or two, and then pour some acid fixing solution (hypo) into the tank. After approximately 15 minutes pour this out and again wash in running water, giving the film a good wash of at least 15 minutes at this point. You can then see how your negatives look because they are finished. Once you have wiped off the excess water

*Enjoyment of photography can
be greatly increased by
a nominal investment for the
basic materials needed
to equip your own darkroom*

The process for developing film is easy to learn. Spooling the film onto a reel is not difficult but it has to be done in total darkness. You should practice doing this until it is easy for you to do it literally blindfolded.

You can develop your own films with this simple layout—tank, thermometer, and two chemical solutions. The sheet of instructions that comes with your film will tell you all you will have to know about actual developing time.

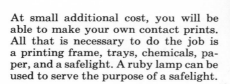

At small additional cost, you will be able to make your own contact prints. All that is necessary to do the job is a printing frame, trays, chemicals, paper, and a safelight. A ruby lamp can be used to serve the purpose of a safelight.

and allowed them to dry thoroughly you can order or make prints from them.

Equipment

Equipment needed for this operation includes:

One developing tank and reel

Photographic thermometer

Box or bottle of prepared developer. The powder type in the box is dissolved in a specified amount of water while the bottled developer is diluted to make the proper solution. Some developers can be used repeatedly while others are discarded after one use.

Box of acid fixing powder, commonly called hypo. Enough to make a gallon of solution costs less than a dollar, and it can be used over and over many times.

The developing process is so simple that anyone can do it. There is only one thing that has to be learned and that is how to spool the film onto the reel that goes in the tank. This is not in itself difficult but it has to be done in total darkness and it is a good idea to practice the loading of the reel so that you can do it literally blindfolded. Outdated film which you can pick up at bargain prices in many stores will serve for practice in how to spool film correctly.

Many amateurs do their own developing, and even carry this kind of "darkroom" with them when they travel so they can check results without delay. The main reason, though is because this can produce superior results. You can go by the book to get fine grain or ultra speed, and can match your picture-taking technique with your developing in a way that will give you complete control of your photography—a control you cannot get otherwise.

Getting extra film speed

It has been noted that film can be speeded up in development. You are not likely to get this kind of specialized service in the ordinary commercial course of events, but you can get extra film speed if you develop your own films and you can get it quite easily. If you use as your developer the old stand-by known as D-76, the normal development time for film rated at 400 ASA is 8 minutes at 68 degrees F. But by increasing the developing time to 10 minutes at 70 degrees you can push the film speed to 650 ASA. That's a big jump, too, the equivalent of increasing the speed of an f/2 lens to f/1.5.

The instruction sheets that come with film tell you all you will need to know about developing that particular type and there are books on the subject if you want to go further into the matter. All this literature emphasizes a vital point: if you want superior negatives follow instructions carefully. If 68 degrees is called for, don't make it 70 or even 69. If developing time is supposed to be 8 minutes, don't make it 6 or 9. Unless, of course, you are trying for some special effect.

Contact prints

If you wish to carry your darkroom work a bit further, to get contact prints so you can better see what results you obtained, you will need a few more pieces of equipment, and room in which to use it. You will need a safelight—a ruby-colored bulb will do—three enameled or hard rubber trays, a frame to hold negatives and sensitized paper; and some prepared developer that you mix with water. (The most widely used paper developer is called D-72.) These things plus the same type of acid fixing bath you used for your films are all you need.

In one tray you pour your developing solution, water goes in the second tray, and acid fixing solution goes in the third. Then turn out the room light and light the safelight, which will permit you to see the picture as it takes shape on the paper, without fogging it. You are now ready to make a print. Place the negative in the frame, with the glossy side facing the glass and against it place a piece of sensitized paper with the emulsion side facing the negative. (If you have any doubts as to which side contains the emulsion, you can tell from the way the paper curves. The emulsion is on inner side of curving paper.)

When film and paper are together, set the back of the frame in place and secure it. Then turn on a light—a white 60-watt bulb permits easy-to-measure exposure time—and hold the frame a foot or so away from it so that it strikes the glass front of the printing frame. Expose for several seconds—the exact amount of time for a good print is a matter of trial and error—and then turn off the light. Remove the paper from the frame and place it in the developer. The image will slowly appear: if it jumps up too suddenly you gave it too much exposure when you held the frame to the light; if it appears too slowly and does not build up to a good image you did not give it enough exposure. When the image builds up fully, remove the print from the developer and swish it around in the water to remove as much of the chemical as possible, and then place it in the acid fixing bath. In a few seconds you can turn on the light and see what you have. As in the case of developing film, it is important that prints be thoroughly washed after coming out of the acid fixing bath since in time any trace of hypo that remains will cause them to discolor.

With a pretty small investment you have thus gone full circle, not only taking pictures but making them too. And somehow such pictures provide a lot more satisfaction than those printed by some outside party. In the course of making them, too, you cannot help but learn some valuable lessons about photography. And one other advantage is that with this simple darkroom you get superior results and you can get them quickly. Within a half hour you can see negatives of the pictures you have taken, and minutes after the negatives are fully dry you will be able to see prints of your handiwork.

Enlarging. In case you should want to venture further, the final step is enlarging. This calls for only two changes in contact procedure. Instead of a printing frame, you use an enlarger, so that you can make pictures of any size instead of using contact printing paper you use enlarging paper, which comes in various sizes—4 by 5, 5 by 7, 8 by 10, and even larger.

In enlarging you put your negative into a holder which slips into the enlarger and you project an image on an easel. When you get it sharp by focusing, you insert a piece of enlarging paper in the easel and project the image on the sensitized surface. Here, as in the case of contact printing, a bit of trial and error is usually necessary to get an idea of how long you should expose the paper, but after it is exposed you develop it and fix it precisely in the same manner as you did the contact prints.

In addition to the satisfaction of accomplishing something worth-while, enlarging gives you other advantages. It permits you to manipulate your pictures, cropping them so you use the most effective parts, straightening lines that may have been distorted in the negative, and correcting for overexposure and underexposure, a trick easy to do with special papers that give more or less contrast. But in an enlarged print you get a picture with far more impact than any you find in a small picture, and, highly important to most people, it's an economical way of getting top-flight pictures.

Chapter 16

Accessories

There are few amateur photographers who have not gazed enviously at the enticing array of accessories in camera stores, dreaming of pictures they could get if only they had all those different lenses, the cameras with all sorts of built-in controls, the powerful electronic flash outfits and the remote control apparatus.

Certainly such equipment would produce some wonderful pictures but how many people can afford such elaborate gadgets? And besides, maybe they are not as essential as you think. Using other and much cheaper accessories it is often possible to get pictures that compare quite favorably with those produced with costly equipment.

Take the matter of lenses. Everyone would like to own a camera with an f/2 or an f/1.5 lens to get pictures under difficult lighting conditions, but as you know there is another way of getting sufficient light on your film if you have to use a small aperture. You simply take the picture at a slower shutter speed, and you might be surprised at how well you can make out, by doing just that.

Here's a case in point. Let's say you are going to see a play being presented at your local high school. You'd like to take pictures but you have been informed that no flash will be allowed. If you had a camera with one of those big lenses you'd have no trouble but unfortunately your old folding camera has only an f/7.7 lens, and you know that the lighting in the school auditorium is not as brilliant as it might be. In fact, a friend who has attended rehearsals has told you

There is no need to load up with
accessories to get good
pictures but a filter or other item
often means better pictures

that his exposure meter showed that it would take an f/2 lens opening to get pictures at 1/125 of a second shutter speed.

Is the situation hopeless? Not at all. Simply use a tripod. That plus your old camera loaded with the fastest film you can get, and you are assured of properly exposed pictures. If you recall the simple f-number formula, by squaring and comparing f/2 and f/7.7 you know that your lens is 15 times slower than the f/2. So instead of being able to take pictures at 1/125th of a second you'll just have to slow down your shutter speed to 1/8th of a second.

And that is where the tripod comes in since it is virtually impossible to hand-hold a camera and get sharp pictures at such a slow speed. Further, your camera probably does not even have such a slow speed so you will have to use your B (bulb) stop to make the exposure. This means estimating the exposure, but don't let that worry you. Open and close the shutter quickly and you'll come close enough. However, to do this successfully calls for a firm support—a tripod. You won't want to burden yourself with a big, heavy model, especially at a performance such as this school play. Your choice should be one of those sturdy, lightweight models whose legs fold up small enough so the entire outfit can be strapped to the side of a gadget bag. Such a tripod can be set up between your legs when you settle yourself to see the play, and it won't be conspicuous nor will it get in anyone's way. Somewhat handier is the collapsible one-legged "unipod" fitted with a ball-top.

You might consider another type of camera holder, one with a clamp which permits you to fasten it almost anywhere, and with a tilt-top arrangement which allows you to move the camera in any position. Such a holder could be fastened to the seat in front of you (if the person sitting there has no objection) but there's one thing to remember in taking pictures in this way —watch out that the person in the seat ahead

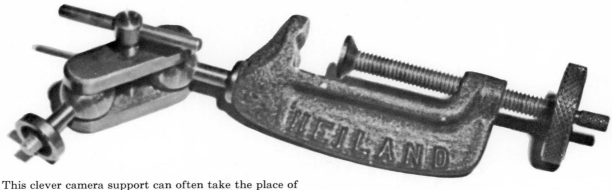

This clever camera support can often take the place of a tripod. The clamp serves to hold it securely and an ingenious top locks the camera in any desired position.

doesn't shift position to get in the way of the camera. And remember, too, that slow shutter speeds mean you'll have to take your pictures when the members of the cast are not moving about, otherwise you'll probably get a blur.

This is not the only kind of situation in which a tripod can come in handy. If it were possible or convenient to use a tripod for all your pictures you'd notice a marked improvement in them. Maybe "sharp improvement" would be a more accurate phrase because the pictures would certainly be sharper than the ones you ordinarily get. Too, there's something about a tripod that makes a photographer take a little more time and care in getting his pictures, and that can make a great difference.

Not many people look upon film as an accessory but it may be considered as such, and a pretty versatile accessory it is, too. Just as a tripod can substitute for a high speed lens worth a hundred dollars or more, so film can give you pictures you may not realize are within the scope of the camera you now own.

High speed films are readily available but some people are not aware that they can buy films that, in effect, put a larger lens on their camera. This is not to detract from the merits of the slower films; in most cases such films are preferable for amateur pictures. But there are occasions when a fast film can produce results otherwise impossible to obtain, so it might be worth-while to ask your dealer about the availability of such films and do a little experimenting with them. Relatively few amateurs—even those who know about super-speed films—realize that there is a way of making those fast films even faster.

Eastman's Tri-X, for example, has a speed rating of 400 ASA, which is pretty fast, but even this can be speeded up considerably merely by developing it a bit longer. Some professionals, notably those who work for the big picture magazines, make frequent use of this technique, and if they want the utmost in film speed they use special developers which can speed up Tri-X from its usual 400 ASA to 1250 ASA. The significance of this is apparent if you think of this speed-up in connection with that venture into theatrical photography. Using 400 ASA film you would have had to shoot your pictures at 1/8 of a second, but if you pushed the speed to 1250 in development you could have taken your pictures at 1/30th of a second.

Infrared film. An unusual kind of film which might rate as an accessory because of the unusual pictures it permits is called infrared. With infrared film you can get pictures of a believe-it-or-not nature. You can, for example, take pictures in the dark without the subjects' knowledge since the light used for picture-taking is invisible, coming from the extreme red, or infrared, end of the spectrum. Such pictures are usually made with flash that is heavily filtered to cut out the visible light, and an infrared filter is used over the camera lens. Infrared film can also be used to take pictures of hot objects that show no visible light, such as an electric iron. Since it can see through atmospheric haze it permits pictures of a far distant scene, a scene which may actually be invisible to the eye.

Any film can be made more versatile with filters. Those important accessories are disks of colored glass or gelatin that are attached in front of the lens to screen out certain rays of light so that other rays can be emphasized, providing special effects. Probably the type of filter best known to amateurs is that which is used with black and white film to bring out the clouds in the sky. Such filters are usually yellow or light green, and since they hold back some of the light you have to compensate for this by a longer exposure. The extent to which you have to increase the exposure is known as the filter factor. A yellow filter calls for an exposure double that or-

Photographed without a filter, this distant scene was so obscured by haze that only nearby areas are clear.

A red filter and infrared film penetrated the haze, thus allowing the camera to see farther than the human eye.

dinarily required so the filter factor is two. A red filter, which puts exaggerated clouds in dark sky or which makes buildings stand out against such darkened skies as though etched, requires eight times the normal exposure, so the filter factor to be used in this case is eight.

However, there are many filters, and they serve many purposes. Users of color film know that they have to use filters when they use indoor film outdoors or vice versa, but there are other filters that can improve your color pictures. One that provides very interesting effects is called a polarizing filter. With it you can literally adjust the color of the sky, making it light or dark, and with it you can prevent glare and reflections. A polarizing filter is effective with black and white film too. There are ultraviolet absorbing filters that cut through haze, and there are even filters that will slow down fast film and lenses without affecting the relationship between the colors. Called neutral density filters they permit you to use very fast film outdoors in brilliant light without overexposure.

On the subject of light and lenses, these two sometimes combine to cause flare which can spoil a good picture. To prevent this a lens shade is essential. This inexpensive accessory keeps stray rays of light from striking your camera lens, and it isn't necessary to point your camera directly at a bright light to get flare. A few random rays can play havoc with the crispness that is the mark of a good photograph.

Throughout this book there have been repeated references to long focus lenses and wide-angle lenses, and how they can expand the scope of your picture-taking. If your camera will take such lenses and you can afford them they can be valu-able indeed. However, it is possible to get the same general effect with supplementary lenses that you can attach to your normal lens to open up or narrow down its angle.

Supplementary lenses

Other supplementary lenses that have added advantages of being inexpensive, will permit you to get close-ups. These break the space barrier since with them you can come a lot closer than the six or ten feet minimum distance required by so many cameras. Serving much as lenses in eyeglasses used for reading type without having it appear blurred, these lenses are variously called portrait, portra or proxar lenses and come in different strengths or powers. Each is good for a specified range, down to approximately ten inches. They slip on over the regular lens, but in using them make sure that the subject is lined up so it is precisely centered and at the right distance from the camera.

If your camera happens to be a single lens reflex you can open up a whole new world of photography by means of a bellows attachment that goes between the camera body and the lens. This permits extreme close-ups so that you can photograph tiny objects. With it you can make insects appear monstrous, copy items in stamp and coin collections.

When you engage in any sort of photography where camera movement must be avoided, an important (and inexpensive) accessory is a cable release. Many amateurs consider this a relic of the dark ages of photography but it serves a valuable purpose in providing a means of tripping the shutter gently without jarring the cam-

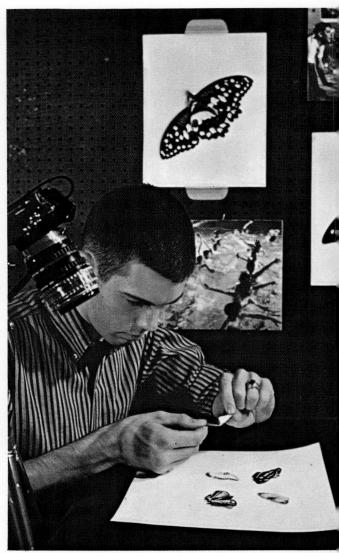

Hobbyists can photograph their coins, and biological specimens by use of supplementary lenses, extension tubes, and bellows.

era. Some cameras, usually older models, have their shutter releases in awkward places so that it is hard to take a picture without a possibility of jerking the camera. But even when the release button is conveniently placed there are some amateurs who feel that the way to get a good exposure is to whack it with vigor. The result is likely to be a picture that has an over-all blur.

Many expensive cameras come equipped with a built-in self-timer that permits a person to take his own picture, but the same effect can be achieved with a self-timing device that you can attach in a jiffy when you need it. Many amateurs prefer the detachable type, not only because it costs only a few dollars but they see no point in having their camera mechanism complicated with a device that they are not likely to use very often. In defense of the built-in release it might be mentioned that photographers engaged in critical work sometimes use it to prevent the transmission of even the slightest tremor in delicate, high magnification work.

If you have a single lens reflex or coupled range finder camera that will take such an accessory, a bellows extension such as this gives camera a new dimension. Not only can it be used for very close work but with appropriate lenses it can also give telephoto pictures. Providing still greater versatility, when used in connection with special holder it permits copying of color slides.

Exposure meters are so essential to good pictures that an increasing number of cameras have them built in and quite often coupled so that they set the exposure automatically. This particular type uses a battery-powered cadmium sulphide cell to sense the amount of the available light.

Exposure meters. Exposure meters were once used solely by professionals and advanced amateurs who could afford their high price, but today things are different, and many cameras have meters built in. However, if yours does not have a meter you can get one for a few dollars and there are few better investments in photography. The operation is simple. A sensitive cell, either selenium or cadmium sulphide, reacts to the light and causes a needle to move on a scale to show you how much light there is. Another scale trans-

lates this into how much of an exposure you should give the picture. Once you master this technique your overexposed and underexposed pictures should decline to the vanishing point.

Flash guns, too, are such an integral part of photography that they are often not considered as accessories. Certainly they are not when they are built into the camera, but if you are considering a flash gun as a separate unit there are a few things to keep in mind. The type that fastens firmly to the camera without a cord will probably

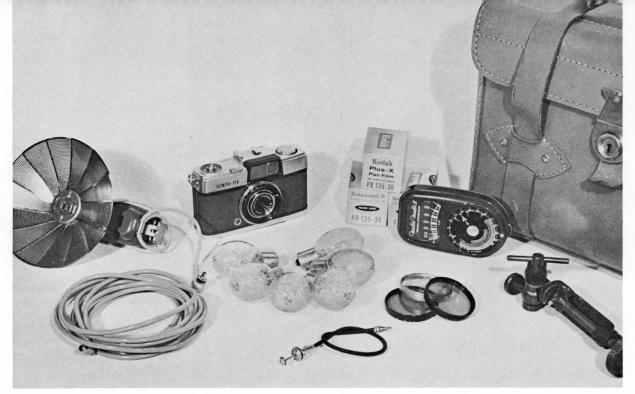

A well-stocked camera case will have, besides a camera, a flash gun and extension cord, plenty of film and flash bulbs, exposure meter, filters, cable release and camera clamp or tripod. Get a bag that is sized right for you.

provide better electric contacts with less chance of failure, but a flash gun that can be removed from the camera and then fired from different positions will probably give you better pictures.

As you know, when you can hold the flash gun away from the camera at different angles you can get better effects than when you shoot your flash dead ahead. This idea can be given greater scope through the use of extension cords that permit you to fire flash bulbs at distances up to 20 feet. This makes it possible for you to get all sorts of unusual lighting effects. You can place your subject on a stairway and set off the flash from the head of the stairs, taking the picture from below. Or you can have your subject in one room, together with the light, while you shoot from another room, using the doorway as a frame.

Too, a detachable flash gun permits you to bounce your light to get natural lighting effects, and if you want to employ a variation of this technique select a flash gun whose reflector can be removed or folded, fanlike, out of the way. With such a unit you can take what are called bare-bulb pictures. Photographs taken in this manner have a soft, pleasant appearance.

Electronic flash. If you take or plan to take many flash pictures an electronic flash outfit may be a good investment. If you are like most amateurs you will probably prefer the portable transistorized type. These give you pictures at a battery cost of two or three cents a picture as against three or four times that when you use flash bulbs. But that is not the whole story. The initial cost of an electronic flash unit is far higher than that of a conventional flash gun so don't make this large investment if you take relatively few pictures.

These are some of the more important accessories that will help you to get better pictures. Now what do you do with all this stuff when you want to take it with you "on location"? You could carry all your odds and ends of film, filters, meter, flash gun and bulbs, in a gadget bag. But here it is easy to go wrong.

Don't do as many amateurs do—buy a bag and then see if it will hold what they want to carry. First take stock of what you will want to carry. One camera or two? Extra lenses? Filters? Flash gun? How many flash bulbs and how much film? Do some figuring and get all these things in one place and see how much bulk they represent. Then take them to camera store where you can be properly fitted with the right kind and size of bag. If you can't find a bag to suit you, a flight bag of the kind made available by airlines may provide at least a good stopgap.

Not a single item mentioned is absolutely necessary to get pictures. Your camera, unadorned with anything but film, will take pictures that will at the very least be adequate. However, if you are interested in better pictures, these accessories will help.

1. Normal lens.

2. Normal lens with 1-plus Portra lens.

3. Normal lens with 2-plus Portra lens.

4. Normal lens with 3-plus Portra lens.

5. Normal lens with 2-plus and 3-plus Portra lenses.

By using portrait or Portra lenses over camera lens you can get close-up pictures to within a few inches of your subject, as shown here. Picture in the upper left hand corner was taken with a camera placed at its normal minimum distance, six feet. By using Portra lenses of different powers it was possible to get pictures of the girl at closer distances until, by combining two Portra lenses, an extreme close-up was obtained. Be careful of a thing called parallax when working at close range. This is caused because the view finder is offset from the lens.

Chapter 17

Better picture tips

To get good pictures it is important to know what not to do as well as what should be done. Obviously a person should understand his camera, just as a motorist should know something about the car he drives and the handyman is expected to know something about the tools he uses. Yet there are many amateur photographers who launch themselves into photography after asking only one question: "Which button do I push?"

Thanks to the simplicity of many cameras, particularly the new automatics, these people get pictures and sometimes good pictures. But there are bound to be failures and even their good pictures could be improved if they took the time to learn about the camera they use.

Nor is it enough to understand the manner in which a camera functions. It is equally important to think in terms of pictures and how they are going to look in the finished form. Photographs can reveal a great deal about the people who took them. Just as no two people see the same thing in precisely the same way, so photographs show different points of view and varying degrees of artistry and originality. To get photographs that show these latter qualities does not call for special equipment or training. The prime essential is learning about the use of the camera you have, and the following check list of better picture tips may help you to achieve that goal.

All the tips for better pictures can be summarized in two rules—learn what your camera can do and then learn what you can do with your camera

1. If you are just getting started in photography and are buying a camera don't select it on the basis of gadgets and gimmicks. Your primary consideration should be the kind of pictures you intend to take, and the camera should be a type that will permit you to get the best results.

2. Having decided on the kind of camera you want, buy the best one you can afford since subsequent "trading up" can be costly.

3. If you already have a camera get to know it better. It will probably give you better pictures than you have been getting. Don't be like many amateurs who constantly change cameras on the theory that the latest model will automatically improve the caliber of their pictures.

4. If you get a new camera read the instructions carefully before you attempt to take a single picture. With the instruction book before you, check every control on the camera and make sure you know its function and how to work it. If anything is not clear ask questions of someone who knows. Then try some "dry runs" without film, going through the motions of taking pictures at different shutter speeds, apertures, and distances.

5. If in the course of trying out the camera, or at any time, some control does not seem to work properly, *never force it*. This could result in a costly and time-consuming repair job.

6. When you have a clear understanding of how your camera works, put your first roll of film in it. If the operation does not proceed smoothly, try it again. Film-loading should be practiced repeatedly, especially if your camera is a type that is not easily loaded. There will be times when you are under tension, in an awkward position, or under other trying conditions. At such times, preliminary practice pays off.

Mistakes can be avoided if you just WATCH OUT

Watch out *when you photograph a tall building. Don't aim camera sharply upwards. This falling-back effect is result*

Watch out *for camera movement. Faster shutter speeds can prevent such errors*

Watch out *for fingers, straps, that get in front of the lens as shutter snaps*

Watch out *for double exposure if you have camera with a manual film advance*

Watch out *for this effect, vignetting, caused by too small lens shade*

Watch out *for glass and bright surfaces that reflect brilliant light back to camera lens*

Watch out *for bright sunlight striking metal or glass. It can mean a hot spot*

Inasmuch as your camera can represent a considerable investment, why not insure it? A floater policy will cover your camera in the event it is lost, stolen, damaged, or destroyed.

7. Use your first roll of film (and your second, third, and fourth) for test purposes. The pictures you take will not only show what your camera can do but will indicate your own limitations. How well can you judge light? If you have an exposure meter can you translate its findings correctly to the camera? At what speeds can you safely take pictures without camera movement? Can you use the view finder to best advantages?

8. Take good care of your equipment. Your camera and the accessories that go with it are precision instruments that should never be subjected to rough and careless usage. A few grains of sand or a few drops of water, especially salt water, can play havoc with a camera, so avoid them. Heat and humidity can harm a camera, too, so be careful how and where you store it. Keep it clean of dirt, corrosion, and fingerprints, but don't overdo matters by constant tinkering and overcleaning. A light touch is indicated, especially around lenses.

9. The foregoing points deal largely with preliminaries, steps that every amateur should take but which they all too often neglect. The first of the positive steps necessary in taking pictures is a simple one: *Take it easy. Avoid rushing a picture by quickly aiming the camera and pushing the shutter release. Give it some thought.*

10. Try to get a fresh slant on whatever it is you are photographing. This does not mean that your pictures should be freakish, but you should try to make them different from and better than other pictures that have been made of the same thing.

11. Try taking them from a different angle. Seen from different viewpoints subjects can take on entirely different aspects. A picture of Main Street taken from the top of a tall building is far different, and probably more interesting, than one taken from street level. And if you were to take a picture of the street as you flew over it in an airplane, it would take on an entirely different character.

12. Put people in your pictures if they belong there. The average person is likely to be more interested in people than in things, and if you can combine them your pictures will probably have more appeal to viewers.

13. Experiment with different kinds of light. You are, after all, working in a medium that has tremendous range, so take advantage of its great variety. Experiment with moonlight or infrared.

14. Give some thought to foregrounds. Here you get into framing and other aspects of composition. The important question is, does the foreground improve the picture? If it does not, try another location. If it does, see if there are ways of making it even more effective.

15. Be careful with those backgrounds. They can improve your pictures but they can also ruin them. Try for backgrounds which will enhance the picture, but if this is impossible you should at least try to minimize a poor or mediocre background by using a large lens aperture to make it as indistinct as possible.

16. Move up close. It is surprising how many diffident amateur photographers there are, people who are reluctant to get close enough to see what is going on and get pictures that would tell the story. Take your cue from news photographers who make it their business to find good vantage points. They know that a close-up picture has impact, with the lens of the camera taking the place of the eyes of the person who sees the picture and who wants to be shown exactly what happened. In the same way, when you take a picture make sure you are close enough to show the important details, even if they are such commonplace things as the freckles on the face of a mischievous child.

17. Keep it simple. One reason for the impact of many close-ups is that they are not cluttered with a lot of extraneous matter, and the viewer can concentrate on what the photographer wants to show him. However, even medium and long shots can sometimes be kept simple if you are careful about the angle from which they are taken and if you make light, background, and foreground work for you, not against you.

18. Follow a definite routine in handling your camera so that you are not all thumbs when that unexpected picture turns up that might be the prize winner you've been after for so long.

19. Keep reading, experimenting, trying. If you are seriously interested in improving your pictures there is a wealth of material available to help you, in the form of books, magazines, and pamphlets. These will give you ideas to work out, and in working them out you will probably evolve some good ideas of your own.

This fine study in black and white is a reminder that interesting pictures are found everywhere, if you just keep looking for them

Many of today's movie cameras have exposure meters that adjust lens apertures automatically as light changes

They also have reflex viewers, and battery-powered motors to transport film. Zoom lenses, supplanting turret-mounted lenses, permit a smooth flow from wide-angle to· telephoto shots. Such lenses are often power-driven

Chapter 18

Movies

Although there are millions of home movie outfits in use, some people believe that film-making is a highly complicated operation. It can be, of course, if it is done the way a professional studio goes about it, but with the kind of equipment sold for amateur use today it is pretty simple. Many amateurs who take both still and motion pictures say movie-making is easier.

A movie camera is basically the same as a still camera. It consists of a container to hold film and a means of transporting it, and it has a lens, shutter and view finder. However, with these similarities go a few differences, notably in operation. The film is transported mechanically, by a spring-driven or electric motor. Shutter speed is constant in most cameras, and you don't have to decide whether to shoot a scene at, say 1/50th or 1/250th of a second. You compensate for varying light conditions by means of an adjustable lens aperture, which can be an iris diaphragm or a series of holes of different diameters.

Amateur movies are usually taken at 16 frames, or pictures, a second, but many cameras give you a choice in this respect, usually from eight to 32 or 64 frames a second. This is primarily to permit special effects, such as taking slow motion pictures. Of course, when you change from 16 frames a second you are also changing the shutter speed. Consult your manual for correct exposure.

The foregoing describes the basic camera but quite often it has various automatic features, all designed to simplify the work of the movie-maker. Many modern cameras have an automatic exposure meter that adjusts the lens aperture instantaneously as the light changes, a reflex viewer that permits the photographer to see exactly what his lens is taking in, and a lens system using a movable lens holder called a turret that gives him a quick choice of wide-angle, normal, or telephoto scenes. One of the greatest boons available to the amateur is the zoom lens that permits him to go smoothly from wide-angle to telephoto shots, and such lenses often come with a further refinement—power drive that moves the lens when you push a button.

Even with all these refinements, movie cameras for nonprofessional use are inexpensive. You can get a good, fully automatic 8-mm movie camera, complete with a zoom lens, for less than you will pay for some of the better grade interchangeable lenses used with 35-mm still cameras.

Today the most popular home movie camera is the 8-mm type and there are approximately 7,000,000 of them in use. The 16-mm movie camera that once dominated the field is now used by only a small percentage of cameramen, most of them serious amateurs or professionals. This switch came about because of economics. Most people considered 16-mm film too expensive and the 8-mm camera was developed, offering the public a great bargain—four pictures for one. It provides this in an ingenious way. Using 16-mm film in 25-foot rolls, it takes pictures on one-half of the film as it runs through the camera. Then the film is flipped over and run through the camera again, and pictures are made on the other half of the film. But that is only half of the economy story. Each of the 16-mm frames gives you two 8-mm pictures on each side, so the 25-foot roll or cartridge of film gives you the equivalent of 100 feet of such film used in a 16-mm camera—approximately four minutes of movies. However, it should be noted that the 16-mm film used in 8-mm cameras has more perforations along the edge, so you can't use conventional 16-mm camera film in the smaller cameras.

Almost all the movies being taken today by amateurs are in color. You would probably have trouble getting black and white film for an 8-mm camera. And this means a further simplification of the movie-making process since the photographer does not have to think in terms of a wide range of film speeds, as the user of a still camera often does. The only thing the movie-maker has to decide concerning film is whether to use outdoor or indoor film. That is no problem as he can use one or the other and employ a filter if his indoor film is to be used outdoors or vice versa. The best procedure is to stick with indoor film, using a filter outside. All around results will be a great deal better.

While it was the low cost of 8-mm film that brought home movies within reach of millions of Americans, manufacturers were canny enough to realize at the outset that cameras using this film had to be made easy to operate and as foolproof as possible, and the price had to be kept low. Here the laws of optics provided an assist because lenses for 8-mm cameras have tremendous depth of field so there is little need to provide for critical focusing, and the small lenses are less expensive than those used in larger cameras.

It should be pointed out though that the 8-mm camera does not provide movies that are equal to those a person can get with a 16-mm camera. If you want to make professional-type movies or fill a huge screen with your pictures you will be better off with the larger camera. However, the person who wants to make movies for his personal use and project them on a screen up to 40 inches in width will find the 8-mm camera fully adequate for his needs. If he uses a modern projector, he can fill a seven-foot screen.

Many people have the idea that in a movie camera the film moves smoothly and steadily from one reel to another. If this were the case the resulting pictures would show a continuous blur. Actually the film is moved through the camera with a series of stop-and-go movements—rapid jerks—providing a series of individual pictures, each one advancing the action. When projected, these pictures are thrown on the screen in a similar stop-and-go manner, and the eye gets the impression of natural movement.

The human viewing mechanism is capable of translating 16 consecutive pictures per second into continuing action, and that is now standard for silent films. If you go in for sound movies, 24 frames a second are recommended.

It is important to understand something about that 16-frames-per-second speed if you want to get good movies, since it is tied in with a pretty slow shutter speed, amounting to 1/30th of a second or even a bit slower, depending on the camera mechanism. Not many people can hold a camera rock-steady at slow shutter speeds, so, to get better and sharper movies, use a support or hold yourself as steady as possible.

Action

This raises the important point that the subjects being filmed should supply the action, not the photographer. You will get superior pictures if you will always keep that in mind. It is easy to tell the novice movie-maker from the way he handles his camera. This bundle of nervous energy takes his pictures in short, machine-gun-like bursts, he waves the camera from one side to the other and up and down, and to supply another dimension he may even walk around as he shoots his pictures. Since this kind of photographer is not inclined to discard anything he ever shoots and projects his films in toto, results are hard on viewers. They will be treated to blurs, streaks of various hues, and disconnected scenes that go up, down, sideways, and on the diagonal.

Compare this sort of photography with what professional cameramen give you on a theater screen or a TV set. Everything is done smoothly and if the camera is moved the movement is almost imperceptible. Enough time is given to each scene so that it registers fully, without becoming tiresome, and the viewer is kept intrigued by being given a constant change of perspective. He is given long shots, medium shots, and close-ups, combined so that he has a complete visual understanding of what is set before him.

This procedure is essential whether the movie camera is being used to film movie stars or a Little Leaguer at bat. In the latter case you can safely go on the assumption that Johnny is going to supply plenty of action, and if your camera is equipped with different lenses you will not only get action but a variety of it. Your wide-angle lens will show the entire diamond and relate Johnny to the other players. The normal lens will catch Johnny, all of him, as he makes his first wild swing, while the telephoto will register his disgust and then his taut chin as he gets set for the next pitch. Then with the normal lens or the wide-angle you can show him as he wallops the ball and rounds the bases for a home run.

The person viewing these pictures will find them more interesting than the all-too-common variety taken in short spurts, with the same lens and from the same position, and with the camera moved almost as vigorously as Johnny's bat. A cautionary note may be in order for those who have a zoom lens. This optical marvel will give you a wonderful choice of angles but don't overdo it. Some movie-makers zip their zoom lenses in and out with such frequency that the results are as annoying as constant and rapid "panning."

A common fault of amateur movies is the result of mistaken notions of economy. Since film costs money some photographers try to save by making their scenes too short. Eight-mm film is inexpensive and it is far wiser to overshoot than to take scenes that are too brief. How long should a scene be? It should be long enough to do the job or tell the story. It is common practice to use signs or other reading matter as movie titles. You won't need much footage to film a highway marker that merely indicates that you are traveling on Route 66 or are on the Garden State Parkway. However, if you come to a marker that describes an important historical event that took place at this spot, take enough time to shoot it so that when it is flashed on the screen viewers will have ample time to digest the message.

Experts say that no scene should be shorter

than five seconds nor should it be longer than 15 seconds, with ten seconds a good average. It's a good rule, though not inflexible, but be sure you know how to count seconds since a second is longer than most people think it is.

What kind of movies should a person take? You can get lifeless pictures with a movie camera as well as with still cameras, and many people go in for movies of this type. You've probably seen such films. A typical scene shows people lined up staring at the camera and on signal a hand waves, a finger is pointed at the camera, or a face breaks into a self-conscious grin.

There is no law against this kind of movie photography but since you paid to get action in your pictures why cheat yourself? And why cheat the people who will see the pictures?

Plan a sequence

As with still pictures, a little planning will pay big dividends and the time to plan your pictures is before you take camera in hand. This is not to suggest that you have to write a scenario and rehearse your subjects before you take any movies. Sometimes that is warranted but usually you will get excellent results if you simply arrange things so that your subjects have something to do that they will find more interesting than the fact that they are being photographed. For example, it doesn't take much planning to know what will happen if you put some children in bathing suits and give them a garden hose to play with. Nor do you have to write a scenario to get amusing pictures when you give youngsters some generous slices of cake liberally coated with chocolate icing.

However, try to work out some sort of a sequence so that your pictures will have a logical beginning and end. It is jarring to viewers when you give them a series of disconnected scenes, and it is even more annoying when you start your movie without any sort of introduction and end it as though you had run out of film.

As an example of how this happens, home movie makers will often suddenly remember on Christmas Day that this is a good opportunity to get some interesting pictures. So the camera is taken down from the shelf and some film is exposed showing the children midway through the opening of their presents. Eventually this particular scene will be projected following some unrelated footage, possibly showing children swimming in a pool, and following it may come a few feet of film showing skiers coming down a slope.

A good film of the Christmas holiday calls for different treatment. Just as the holiday begins well before December 25th, so should your movie. You can establish that point by starting your film with a shot showing a calendar turned to the appropriate date. Included in the early part of your movie should be such preliminary activities as greeting cards being addressed, cookies being baked, packages being wrapped, the tree being brought home, and so on. The children can be photographed as they compose their letters to Santa Claus and talk to that kindly gentleman, and as they hang up their stockings for his attention on Christmas Eve.

On the big day a chronological sequence of shots is indicated. Show the children getting up, coming downstairs, and then bursting into the room to see the tree and the presents underneath it. Since this will probably be the high spot of the day make the most of it by taking your pictures from various positions employing different angles. Close-ups are important to show facial expressions and little hands busy with toys, and don't neglect to show Sally trying on her lovely new bathrobe and Jimmy making something with his new building blocks.

Nor should the film end abruptly at this point. Follow through, to show the family at dinner, the friends who come to visit, the children being chased off to bed, and the grownups resting after the day's excitement.

No movie should ever end as though your last foot of film had suddenly coursed through the camera or as though the spring had run down. Nor is that sort of thing necessary since things usually have a way of coming to natural conclusions. A movie of a wedding supplies its own ending as the newlyweds hurry off in their car. At a football game a shot of the final score on the big board can wrap up the story. The end of a trip can be dramatized by showing the luggage being carried into your home.

You will find your movies getting better when you reach the stage where you think of your film in terms of how it will look when projected, instead of merely taking haphazard shots without giving much thought to the end result. Will the scene you are about to shoot advance the story you are trying to tell or not? If the latter, can it be taken in some other way so that it will be appropriate? Will five or ten seconds be enough time to do a particular scene justice? Will a close-up of that youngster or that balloon peddler fit into the continuity of the parade film you are making? Should you shoot that waterfall with a wide-angle lens or should you use a telephoto lens to show the boiling torrent at the bottom of the gorge? Or should you take it both ways?

There are always a lot of questions you can ask yourself as you take movies, and the very fact that you are asking questions indicates that you are improving. Too much film is shot without any thought of the picture as it will be projected.

Editing

Just as a darkroom can often salvage the mistakes and shortcomings of still photographers, so a bit of post-shooting work can often make a good movie out of material that would otherwise

The 16-mm film used in 8-mm camera gives four pictures a frame; projects well on 40-inch-wide screen.

underexposed, any footage that shows camera movement, and whatever else is technically poor. The higher your standards in this respect the better your movies will be.

The next step is to rearrange the footage you have available so that your film has the proper continuity, with a logical beginning, middle, and end. After this the "pace" of the film must be considered, and here is where you shorten overly long scenes or remove others that get in the way or otherwise interfere with the flow of your story.

Titles. If you want your movies to have a professional touch titles are important and they are usually fitted into the film in the course of the editing process. Here we are thinking in terms of conventional titles rather than the signs and markers that are often taken as part of the film itself to provide identification. Many amateurs forego titles for their films, thinking that they are too difficult but this is not necessarily so. The Christmas film you make can employ children's alphabet blocks for title-making, or the titles can be typed on cards decorated with sprigs of balsam or holly. Or, if something more professional is wanted, sets of title letters are available or you can get a complete titling outfit.

Whatever method you use, make and employ your titles with care. Those that are well done can enhance any home movie and give it a professional touch while sloppily done titles are worse than none. If you have artistic friends, enlist their help to provide decorative touches and the lettering. Shooting the titles calls only for reasonable care. The trick is to make sure that your camera is firmly fixed and focused at the proper distance from the title and that the lens is aimed at the exact center of the title board.

Finally, take a little extra time when you get around to showing your movies to others. Many movie-makers spare no effort to put together a fine film, but then they spoil the effect by the way in which they present their offerings. It only takes a few minutes to set up a projector and a screen, thread the film, and get the image focused and centered on the screen. However, it will make a difference if you spend these few minutes before your audience shows up.

be mediocre. The process is called editing and it is not difficult at all.

Hollywood is well aware of the importance of this aspect of movie-making. Far more film is left on the cutting room floor than "goes into the can." Entire scenes, sequences, and secondary plots are often jettisoned to tighten up a professional movie and give it greater impact. In a small way you can follow Hollywood's example, and all you need are two devices, an editor and a splicer. The former is a means of viewing the film with a minimum of effort so you can decide what has to be done, and the splicer is an inexpensive gadget that holds the film while you cut it and then fasten the ends together.

In editing a movie the first job is to eliminate all the worthless stuff, the film that is over- and

A good rule in shooting movies is to have scenes average ten seconds. Keep camera steady and let the action be provided by the subjects

148

Chapter 19

Language of photography

Photography has a language of its own. In the strange jargon of photography old words take on new and different meanings, brand-new words keep cropping up in print and conversation, and abbreviations and initials are employed when words seem to fail.

You can, of course, take pictures without knowing a single word of this language but it may help if you have at least a glimmering of what all the talk is about. It might someday come in handy to know whether to choose between a fish-eye lens or a zoom, and it certainly won't hurt you to understand what is meant by fast film and fast lenses—and to realize that one is based on ASA ratings and the other on f-numbers. Every photographer should know the difference between a spot and a barn door, and how to use them, along with slaves, in high key work or to prevent chalk and charcoal effects. A person should understand how to avoid lens lice and realize why a bulb squeezer rates only the scorn of the dedicated pro. Further, every amateur worthy of his salt should know what soup is likely to give him the finest grain and he should be able to prove it by jumbo blowups, even though he has to push his negatives to get the proper gamma.

Confusing? Probably. Exaggerated? Not a bit. All these words and phrases are perfectly valid and are used all the time by people who use

cameras, especially those who make their living in photography. So that you can understand what these people say and the things they write, these and other words and phrases are explained in the following abridged photo dictionary.

Acid fixing bath. A solution which fixes, or makes permanent, on film or paper the image brought out in development. Consists of sodium hyposulphite with an acid of some kind added. Often referred to as hypo.

Adapter. A term applied to any of a number of photographic accessories. It may be a mount to hold a supplementary lens or filter. It may be a device to permit the use of Polaroid film in a press camera.

AG bulb. A tiny flash bulb, so small that dozens can easily be carried in a pocket.

Angle of view. The width of the angle included by a particular lens on a given size film. A telephoto or long focus lens has a narrow angle of view. A wide-angle lens covers a wide angle.

Aperture. The lens opening through which light is admitted to the camera. Aperture size is expressed in f-numbers such as f/2.8 or f/8. The larger the f-number the smaller the aperture.

ASA. Abbreviation for American Standards Association, commonly used in connection with film speed or sensitivity. One film will have an ASA rating of 25, while another will have a rating of 400. The former will be relatively slow, the latter very fast or sensitive. The rating is based on standards set by the association.

Understanding the basic terms used in photography won't qualify you as a professional but it will help solve picture-taking problems

151

Automatic camera. One which employs an electronic device to provide the proper exposure. Different methods and degrees of automation are used in various cameras, but fully automatic cameras adjust both diaphragm and shutter speed, and prevent the photographer from taking a picture if there is not enough light.

Available light. Natural light without such artificial assists as flash. Available light photography is a field in which no special lighting is employed, and it usually requires fast film and fast lenses, together with special development.

Back-lighting. A lighting effect that is obtained when the source of illumination is behind the subject and toward the camera. Often used in portraiture, for "halo" effect.

Barn door. Movable deflectors attached to a light to permit adjustment of the beam.

Battery-capacitor. Often abbreviated B-C, it is a source of power for a flash gun. It employs a small dry cell battery in conjunction with a capacitor or condenser. The latter stores the current and releases it in a surge to fire flash bulb.

Between-the-lens shutter. A commonly used shutter that fits between the elements that comprise a camera lens. It has blades of very thin metal which open and close rapidly and it operates with such efficiency that the opening expands immediately to the very edges of the lens. Two well-known shutters of this type are the Compur and the Prontor.

Blowups. A slang term for enlargements.

Bounce light. Indirect light which is obtained by aiming flash at a near-by wall or ceiling instead of pointing it directly at the subject. The wall or ceiling reflects the light evenly giving a more natural effect.

Bracket. A photographer "brackets" his exposure by taking several to make sure of getting one exactly right. If his meter calls for an exposure of 1/100th of a second at f/8, he will take one at that setting, but he will insure himself by "bracketing," taking one providing a bit more exposure and another with a bit less exposure than the meter called for.

Bulb squeezer. A photographer who gives little thought to the kind of picture he is taking, but merely aims his camera and trips the shutter.

Burn up. To overexpose a picture or part of one. Placing a spotlight on a subject or using flash in a poorly designed reflector can cause one to "burn up" a picture so that detail is lost.

Cable release. A flexible wire in a sheath which attaches to shutter release, permitting picture taking with less danger of camera movement.

Camera. A closed box containing an aperture which permits the image of an object to enter to be recorded on light-sensitive material.

Candid. A term used in various ways to indicate pictures with a natural, unposed quality. "Candid pictures" are taken with a "candid camera" the latter usually meaning a small and unobtrusive 35-mm type.

Carrier. A frame for holding a negative in an enlarger or a transparency in a projector.

CdS (Cadmium Sulphide). A small and efficient battery-powered photo cell which has permitted the development of extra-sensitive miniature light meters.

Chalk and charcoal. Excessive contrast in a print which results in unrelieved black and white tones. "Soot and whitewash" is another term used to denote the same effect.

Close-up. A photograph taken at close range.

Color negative film. Color film such as Kodacolor or Anscocolor which gives you a negative from which color prints or slides can be made.

Color reversal film. Notable examples are Kodachrome and Anscochrome. In the course of processing such films a negative image is first obtained. This is reversed to a positive by flashing light on it and then continuing the developing.

Color temperature. A means of measuring the quality of light, color temperature is based on the relationship of a radiating body and the color it emits. Color temperature meters show this, with readings given in the Kelvin scale. Morning sunlight, for example, has a color temperature ranging from 5000 to 5500 degrees K., the color temperature of a 60-watt light bulb is 2800 degrees K., and that of a 250-watt photoflood lamp is 3400 degrees K.

Condenser. In optics a lens system which concentrates light, as in a projector. In electricity, a device which stores energy.

Contact print. A print made by placing a negative in contact with photographic paper, exposing it to light and developing.

Contrast. Variation between light and dark objects in a photograph. A "contrasty" photograph is one that has extreme variations between light and dark areas.

Coupled range finder. An optical-mechanical device which moves the lens into correct focus. The range finder itself is an optical device for measuring distance, but in this usage it is connected to the lens so that as the photographer adjusts it he is automatically focusing his camera.

Definition. The capacity of a lens to give a sharp image by accurately concentrating rays of light without permitting them to spread.

Depth of field. The area, before and behind the point of principal focus, in which all objects appear sufficiently sharp for the photographer's purpose. Varies with distance on which lens is focused, lens aperture (the greater the opening the less the depth) and the degree of enlargement the photographer ultimately desires.

Development. The process of producing a visible image from the latent impression left on film when it is exposed to light.

Diaphragm. Usually called an iris diaphragm, it consists of a series of thin metal leaves attached to a ring in the lens mount, which can be adjusted to enlarge and contract so as to change the aperture, for varying light conditions. The action is much the same as that of the iris of the eye itself.

Documentary. A photograph which portrays something primarily "for the record" and without too much regard for esthetic aspects.

Dodging. A technique used in enlarging to control the image being projected on the paper by the enlarger. Light is held back from certain parts of the picture and concentrated on others.

Easel. A frame which holds photographic paper during the enlarging process.

Electronic flash. Sometimes called strobe or speed light, it is produced by having a powerful electric current surge into a gas-filled tube where it sparks, creating a brilliant flash in that medium.

Emulsion. Sensitized silver salt in suspension used as the coating of film stock, plates, paper and other bases.

Enlarging. A method of obtaining a larger image of a negative or positive by projecting it on a sensitized surface.

EVS. Exposure value scale. See *LVS*.

Exposure. Permitting light to fall on film, contact paper, or enlarging paper. Also refers to the time such sensitized material is exposed, as, a half-second exposure.

Exposure meter. A device, usually employing a photo-electric cell, which measures the amount of light and tells exposure required.

F-numbers. A system used to indicate the diameter of the diaphragm (or lens aperture) being used. It is determined by dividing the focal length of the lens by the diameter of the diaphragm. For example, a lens with a focal length of two inches, and having a diameter of one inch, would be described as an $f/2$ lens. Closing the diaphragm to a half-inch diameter would mean your lens would be set at $f/4$. Figuring it another way, if your exposure meter gave you a reading of $f/4$ and you set your diaphragm to that stop, your lens would be opened to a half-inch diameter.

Fast. A catch-all word applied to film, lenses, and shutter speeds. In the case of film, fast means highly sensitive. Applied to lenses, fast means those with great light-gathering capacity, such as an $f/1.5$, or $f/2$. Fast shutter speeds mean short exposure—1/500th, 1/1000th of a second.

Ferrotype. A smooth metal plate used to give prints a high gloss.

Film. A thin, flexible, transparent material coated with an emulsion; sensitive to light.

Filter. A tinted disk made of glass or gelatin, or a sandwich made of glass and gelatin, placed before the lens to effect the rendering of the various colors, reducing the relative brightness of some and lightening others.

Filter-factor. The use of a filter usually requires a greater exposure. A yellow filter may require three times the normal exposure. In this case the filter factor would be three.

Finder. A sighting device which permits a picture to be framed and studied much as it will appear on the film. Sometimes called a view finder.

Fine grain. See *Grain*.

Fisheye lens. A lens which covers an extremely wide angle, 180 degrees, providing a freakish effect. Usually used to supply a picture of the whole sky in one exposure.

Fixed focus. Under certain conditions it is possible to take pictures without adjusting the focus of the camera. These conditions are met to some extent in a box camera because of the small lens aperture and the requirement that the subject must be ten or twelve feet from the camera. As a result everything beyond this distance is reasonably sharp.

Flare. An optical effect usually caused by internal lens reflections.

Flash bulb. A source of light for photography, provided by igniting electrically fine wire, aluminum foil or gas contained in a glass bulb from which the air has been exhausted.

Flash gun. A device to hold and fire a flash bulb, usually in synchronization with shutter.

Flash tube. The gas-filled tube of an electronic flash outfit which emits a brilliant flash when a charge of electric current is sparked in it.

Flatness. Undesirable quality in a print, showing lack of contrast and snap.

Focal length. The distance from the optical center of the lens to the film when the camera is focused on infinity. The focal length of a lens is usually engraved on the lens mount.

Focal plane shutter. A type of shutter employing a curtain with a slit which passes across and in front of the film to make the exposure.

Focus. To adjust a lens so that the image it projects has maximum sharpness.

Freeze. To stiffen in an unnatural attitude.

Gamma. The degree of contrast of negative.

Grain. An unsightly mottled effect found in films which have been improperly developed or which have an inherent "graininess." It is caused by particles of silver that form into tiny clumps which become noticeable when the picture is enlarged. *Fine grain* is the absence of such clumps, resulting of course in a better picture.

Ground glass. The focusing screen used with certain kinds of cameras on which the photographer can view the picture he intends to take.

Guide number. A number employed in a simple formula which tells you what aperture setting you should use when taking pictures with flash bulbs. The guide number is supplied by the manufacturer of the flash bulb and it is based on its light output. To determine the f-number you should use, it is necessary to consult a chart (usually printed on the flash bulb container) showing film speeds and shutter speeds. On the basis of the film you are using and the shutter speed you plan to use, you are given the proper guide number. To determine the proper f-stop you merely divide this guide number by the distance in feet from flash bulb to subject. If the given guide number is 160 and you are going to stand 10 feet from your subject you should set your diaphragm at f/16. If the guide number is 80 and you are going to stand 10 feet from the subject, the lens should be opened up to f/8.

Halation. A blurriness found in pictures, resulting from the spreading of high lights into the darker areas of the picture.

Half-frame. A miniature camera, or more properly a subminiature, which uses 35-mm film but which takes only half the usual 1 by 1½ inch negative size, so that a 36-exposure roll of film provides 72 pictures.

High key. Light tones in a picture.

Hyperfocal distance. The nearest point on which a particular lens can be focused to produce satisfactory definition at infinity. Varies with focal length and f-stop.

Hypo. Common name for sodium hyposulphite.

Incident light. A term used to differentiate between two methods of light measurement. An incident light reading of an exposure meter requires that the meter be aimed so that it measures the amount of light that is reaching the lens from all sources. On the other hand, a reflected light reading calls for aiming the meter at the subject and measuring the amount of light reflected by it toward the camera.

Infinity. The distance at which light rays from a point source is so great that they may be regarded as parallel. In practice, when the focusing scale of a camera is set at "infinity" everything beyond a certain point (varies with the focal length and aperture) will be in focus.

Infrared. That part of the spectrum beyond the visible red is the invisible infrared region. These rays can be photographed by means of special film used with a deep red filter.

Intensification. A chemical method of building up the silver deposit on an underexposed negative so as to get a printable image.

Kelvin. A measurement of temperature in degrees Centigrade, and covering the color temperature of any given light source.

Latent image. The impression made on light-sensitive material when an exposure is made. Invisible, it takes shape as material developed.

Lens. Glass disks with surfaces of different shapes—concave, convex, plano-concave, etc.—which are usually used in combination to form an image by changing the direction of light rays.

Lens coating. A microscopically thin coating of a metallic substance, such as magnesium fluoride, applied under high vacuum to a lens or other optical surface to increase its efficiency by reducing reflection.

Lens louse. A person who likes to be photographed, to the point of being a nuisance.

Lens shade or **lens hood.** A device which fastens to the lens and protects it from extraneous light.

Light meter. See *Exposure meter*.

Low key. Dark tones in a picture.

LVS, Light value scale. A simplified method of setting the camera for the proper exposure, employed by some cameras and exposure meters. The meter is calibrated with simple numerals to show light intensity, and a dial on the camera carries corresponding numbers. By matching the meter's LVS number with that of the camera, the correct exposure is assured. A similar system is called EVS, Exposure value scale.

Macrophotography. Producing an enlarged image directly on the negative.

Mask. To eliminate part of a picture by framing it off or enlarging only the wanted part.

Matte surface. In photo paper, a smooth or rough surface, as opposed to glossy surface.

Medium shot. A picture made from an intermediate distance.

Millimeter. Usually abbreviated to mm. The metric scale is extensively used in photography, and a millimeter is 1/1000th of a meter or .03937 of an inch. For easy figuring, 25 millimeters equal approximately an inch. Thus, a lens of 50-mm focal length is approximately two inches long.

Mounting. Causing prints to adhere to a card or other material. With transparencies, mounting means placing them in suitable frames.

NC battery. A rechargeable battery in which positive electrode is nickel and the negative electrode is cadmium. Widely used in electronic flash outfits as a source of electricity.

Neutral density filter. A filter which does not affect the rendering of colors but which cuts down the light so that high-speed film may be used in brilliant light.

Negatives. Exposed films or sensitized paper in which lights and shades are reversed.

Objective. The image-forming lens of an optical instrument.

Opaque projector. A device which projects a picture from an opaque surface such as a post card. It does this with mirrors, prisms, and a brilliant light source.

Overexposure. Permitting an excessive amount of light to reach sensitized material.

Open up. To increase the aperture of a lens.

Orthochromatic. Film that is sensitive to yellow, green blue, violet and ultraviolet, but not to red and orange.

Panchromatic. Film that is sensitive to the entire visible spectrum, though less sensitive to red and green than to blue and violet.

Parallax. In photography, this is the difference between what you see in the finder and what is likely to appear on film, when the finder is offset from the lens that takes the picture.

Photomicrography. Using a microscope in conjunction with a camera to get pictures of very small objects.

Plates. Glass plates that have been coated with a light-sensitive material.

Polarized filters. Filters which use the principle of polarized light to eliminate glare from non-metallic objects, and, in color photography, to control the color of the sky.

Polaroid. Usually refers to the picture-in-a-minute-or-less camera, which can develop the picture in the camera as soon as it is taken.

Portrait attachment. A lens which is attached to the regular lens by means of an adapter, and which changes its focus to permit close-up work.

Positive. A reproduction on paper or film of an object in which the shades are as in nature.

Preset diaphragm. A feature found on many lenses used in single lens reflex cameras which permits you to select the aperture you wish to use, open the diaphragm wide for easy focusing, and then close it down to that preselected spot without having to take the camera from your eye. This is carried a step further in the *automatic diaphragm* which closes the diaphragm when the shutter release is pressed.

Printing. The method by which a picture is produced from a negative.

Prints. The finished pictures. Usually refers to contact prints, not enlargements.

Pro. A professional.

Projector. A device consisting of a light source, condenser, lens, and frame for holding negatives or transparencies, to enlarge them onto either a screen or sensitized material. A motion picture projector has a means of advancing the film.

Pushing. In developing films, this refers to a means of getting increased film speed by the use of special formulas or by increasing the time of development.

Range finder. An optical device which measures distance. See *Coupled range finder*.

Recycling. Refers to the recharging of the capacitor of an electronic flash unit, when the batteries pour electricity into the capacitor after it has been discharged by firing.

Recycling time. The time required to refill the capacitor after discharge.

Reduction. A chemical method of correcting overexposure in negatives, to yield a better print.

Reflex camera. A camera which by means of a mirror reflects the image being photographed so it can be seen as it will appear on the film.

Resolving power. The ability of a lens to define images sharply.

Retouching. Treating a negative or a print with a brush, pencil, knife or other instrument to hide defects and otherwise improve it.

Safelight. A light used in a darkroom which is so screened with a filter of red, yellow or green that film or paper may be handled safely in its illumination.

Sharp. Usually refers to a lens, one that has good resolving power.

Shutter. A mechanical device which opens and closes at predetermined speeds to expose film.

Shutter release. The button or lever that trips the shutter of a camera.

Slave lights. Flash units, not directly wired, that operate automatically by means of an electronic control when a master unit is fired.

Slides. Transparencies, either black and white or color, which may be projected.

Slow. Used in connection with film, lenses, shutter speeds. Slow film is not very sensitive. A slow lens is one without much light-gathering capacity. Slow shutter speeds are those of 1/25th of a second or slower.

SLR. Widely used abbreviation for single lens reflex camera.

Soup. Slang for developing solution.

Spec. Speculation. Taking pictures "on spec" means that there is no commitment on the part of the interested party to buy them.

Speed light. See *Electronic flash.*

Spotlight. A light with a concentrated beam.

Stereoscopic. Pertaining to three-dimensional photography.

Stop bath. A mildly acid solution sometimes used for washing negatives of prints after development and before fixing.

Stopping down. Reducing the lens aperture or diaphragm opening.

Stops or **f-stops.** On a diaphragm these are the markings which indicate lens apertures—f/2, f/2.8, f/4.

Stringer. A photographer or reporter who represents a publication whose editorial offices are elsewhere, and who is available to handle assignments in that area.

Strobe. See *Electronic flash.*

Subminiature. Any camera that uses film smaller than the conventional 35-mm. An exception is the half-frame camera which uses such film but does not take pictures in the full-frame size.

Super slides. 2 by 2-inch slides usually made from 127 or 120 film and having a greater film area than that of 35-mm film.

Supplementary lenses. Lenses which are attached by means of an adapter to the regular lens to change its focus to permit either close-up or long focus work.

Sync, Synchronization. Usually refers to the firing of flash, with the shutter synchronized to open when the flash reaches its peak brilliance.

Tanks. Light-tight tanks in which films may be developed in light.

Telephoto lens. A lens of extremely long focal length which increases the size of the image. In effect, a telephoto lens is a telescope which magnifies distant objects on the film.

Toning. Changing the color of a photographic print by chemical means.

Trimming. Cutting a print to eliminate unwanted and extraneous matter and improve the composition of the picture.

Tripod. A three-legged stand designed to hold a camera steady.

Ultraminiature camera. See *Subminiature.*

Ultraviolet. One end of the solar spectrum which, though invisible, has an effect on photographic film.

Underexposure. When insufficient light has been given to film, so that a "thin" or transparent negative results when black and white film is used, dark transparency when color is used.

View finder. See *Finder.*

Wide-angle lens. A lens of short focal length. Covers a wider angle than conventional lens.

Wink light. A light designed for use with the Polaroid camera. Less brilliant than conventional flash it provides ample light for the fast films available for the Polaroid camera.

Zoom lens. A lens whose focal length can be varied so that the user can go smoothly from wide angle to telephoto by turning or extending the lens barrel. A further advantage is that the focal length is changed smoothly and continuously, not in steps.

Look for picture possibilities in the most unlikely places and often you will be rewarded with pictures that will rival the best that might come from an artist's palette

INDEX

ACKNOWLEDGMENTS

We wish to express our thanks to the following firms for providing photographs, drawings, and technical assistance in the preparation of **Photography for your family.**

Ansco, General Aniline & Film Corporation, New York, New York • Argus, Inc., Chicago, Illinois
Eastman Kodak Company, Rochester, New York • Polaroid Corporation, Cambridge, Massachusetts

PICTURE CREDITS

Front Cover . . . . Eastman Kodak
Endpapers . . . . Bill Wittkowski

Page
8 . . . . Vivienne Lapham
9 . . . . Eastman Kodak
10 . . . . Joan Liffring
11 . . . . Eastman Kodak
12 (top) . . . . Richard Royer
12 (center) . . . . Eastman Kodak
12 (bottom) . . . . Eastman Kodak
13 . . . . Eastman Kodak
15 . . . . Eastman Kodak
16 (top) . . . . Eastman Kodak
16 (center) . . . . Harvey Caplin
16 (bottom) . . . . Eastman Kodak
17 (top) . . . . Eastman Kodak
17 (center) . . . . Eastman Kodak
17 (bottom) . . . . Clark Dean,
             Infinity Inc.
18 . . . . Donald Tulloch
19 (top) . . . . Eastman Kodak
19 (center) . . . . Eastman Kodak
19 (bottom) . . . . . Joseph C. Keeley
20 (top) . . . . Wm. Hopkins
20 (bottom) . . . . Marion Pease
21 . . . . Charles Pearson
22 . . . . Ansco
23 . . . . Vincent Maselli
25 . . . . Larry Helton
26 (top) . . . . Eastman Kodak
26 (bottom, left) . . . . Richard Hufnagle
26 (bottom, right) . . . . Bob Towers
27 (top) . . . . Harvey Caplin
27 (center) . . . . Ozzie Sweet
27 (bottom) . . . . Eastman Kodak
29 . . . . Polaroid Corporation
30 . . . . Eastman Kodak
31 . . . . Richard Royer
32 . . . . Eastman Kodak
33 . . . . Eastman Kodak
34 (top) . . . . Eastman Kodak
34 (center) . . . . Richard Royer
34 (bottom) . . . . Eastman Kodak
35 . . . . Eastman Kodak
36 . . . . Eastman Kodak
37 . . . . Eastman Kodak
38 . . . . Eastman Kodak
39 . . . . Eastman Kodak
40 . . . . Hedrich-Blessing
41 . . . . John Rogers
42 (top) . . . . Clark Dean, Infinity Inc.
42 (center) . . . . Bill Hedrich,
             Hedrich-Blessing

42 (bottom) . . . . Bill Hedrich,
             Hedrich-Blessing
43 Bill Hedrich . . . . . Hedrich-Blessing
44 (top, right) . . . . . Frank Scherschel
44 (top, left) . . . . Wm. Hopkins
44 (bottom) . . . . Wm. Maris
45 (top) . . . . Jerry Cooke
45 (bottom) . . . . G. Suter,
             Hedrich-Blessing
46 . . . . Wm. Hopkins
47 . . . . James Herrlin
48 (top) . . . . Warren Reynolds,
             Infinity Inc.
48 (center) . . . . James Herrlin
48 (bottom) . . . . Cleve Lesh
49 (top) . . . . Wm. Hopkins
49 (center) . . . . Wm. Hopkins
49 (lower left) . . . . Kranzten
49 (lower right) . . . . Wm. Hopkins
50 . . . . Wm. Hopkins
51 . . . . Warren Reynolds, Infinity Inc.
52 . . . . Joseph C. Keeley
53 . . . . Larry Helton
54 . . . . Joseph C. Keeley
55 . . . . Ansco
56 . . . . Joseph C. Keeley
57 . . . . Joseph C. Keeley
58 . . . . Joseph C. Keeley
59 . . . . Ansco
60 . . . . Ray Atkeson
61 . . . . Eastman Kodak
62 (top) . . . . Richard Royer
62 (center) . . . . Richard Royer
62 (bottom) . . Great Northern Railway
63 (top) . . . . Eastman Kodak
63 (bottom) . . . . Maynard Reece
64 (top, left) . . . . Eastman Kodak
64 (top, right) . . . . Richard Royer
64 (bottom) . . . . Harvey Caplin
65 (top) . . . . Wm. R. Wilson
65 (bottom) . . . . Richard Royer
66 . . . . Ray Woods
68 . . . . Ray Woods
69 . . . . Ray Woods
70 (top) . . . . Ray Atkeson
70 (center) . . . . Richard Royer
70 (bottom) . . . . Ray Atkeson
71 (top) . . . . Richard Royer
71 (bottom) . . . . Eastman Kodak
72 . . . . Joseph C. Keeley
73 . . . . Joseph C. Keeley
74 . . . . Wm. Hopkins
75 . . . . Joseph C. Keeley
76 (top, left) . . . . Eastman Kodak

76 (top, right) . . . . Wm. Hopkins
76 (bottom) . . . . Eastman Kodak
77 (top) . . . . Wm. Hopkins
77 (bottom) . . . . Ray Woods
79 (bottom, left) . . . . Wm. Hopkins
79 (bottom, right) . . . . Ansco
80 (top) . . . . Joseph C. Keeley
80 (bottom) . . . . Szanik
81 (top, right) . . . . Wm. Hopkins
81 (center) . . . . Kranzten
81 (bottom) . . . . Ansco
83 . . . . Wm. Hopkins
84 . . . . Eastman Kodak
85 . . . . Volkswagen of America
86 (top) . . . . Ray Woods
86 (bottom) . . . . Larry Helton
87 . . . . Ray Woods
89 . . . . Joseph C. Keeley
94 . . . . Larry Helton
99 . . . . George Eastman House
101 . . . . Eastman Kodak
102 (center) . . . . Joseph C. Keeley
102 (bottom) . . . . Joseph C. Keeley
103 (top, left) . . . . Joseph C. Keeley
103 (top, right) . . . . Joseph C. Keeley
103 (center) . . . . Ansco
103 (bottom, left) . . . . Ansco
103 (bottom, right) . . . . Ansco
104 . . . . Joseph C. Keeley
105 . . . . Joseph C. Keeley
106 . . . . Benn Mitchell
113 . . . . Harvey Caplin
114 . . . . Polaroid Corporation
115 . . . . George Eastman House
119 . . . . Morley Baer
120 . . . . Ray Woods
121 . . . . Joseph C. Keeley
122 . . . . Eastman Kodak
123 . . . . Eastman Kodak
125 . . . . James Autry
127 . . . . Eastman Kodak
130 . . . . Ray Woods
133 . . . . Eastman Kodak
134 (top) . . . . Eastman Kodak
134 (center) . . . . Jerry Cooke
137 . . . . Eastman Kodak
138 . . . . James Autry
140 . . . . Joseph C. Keeley
141 . . . . Joseph C. Keeley
143 . . . . Ray Woods
148 . . . . Eastman Kodak
149 . . . . Eastman Kodak
150 . . . . Rada Photography
157 . . . . Ray Woods